NO ONE CAME TO TAOS TO BE JEWISH

BRUCE GROSSMAN

No One Came to Taos to Be Jewish

Copyright © 2022 by Bruce Grossman

All rights reserved. No part of this book may be reproduced, scanned, or distributed in any printed or electronic form without permission. Please do not participate in or encourage piracy of copyrighted material in violation of the author's rights. Purchase only authorized editions.

Cover image, "Taos Mountain," pastel,
cindygrossmanpastels.com
Copyright © 2022

Order books from the author or Nighthawk Press,
or purchase through Amazon.com.

ISBN: 978-1-7378109-5-7

An imprint of Nighthawk Press
P.O. Box 1222
Taos, NM 87571
nighthawkpress.com

For Ron Kalom,
The Kotzker de Taos

Table of Contents

Foreword by Karl Halpert vii

Introduction xi

Part 1, Back to the Garden
My Taos Story 3

Part 2, The Taos Rabbis
Rabbi Chavah Carp 45
Rabbi Judith HaLevy 53
The Kotzker de Taos, Ron Kalom 65

Part 3, The Gatherings
B'nai Shalom Havurah 85
The Taos Minyan 95
The Taos Jewish Center 111
The Eretz Shalom Cemetery 143

Foreword

I was pleased when Bruce Grossman asked me to write a few words to preface his warm and insightful book, *No One Came to Taos to Be Jewish*. He coined this phrase years ago, and it left a mark on me. I grew up in a 1960s shtetl of Conservative Judaism. The assimilation of my grandparents was complete, and we lived prosperously in a gentle, cobble-stoned New England town, nicknamed "Forest City" for its tree-lined streets. I didn't do anything or go anywhere to be Jewish. I knew who I was. I had friends in catechism and friends in Hebrew school. We all played ball together, and Sandy Koufax made me proud to be Jewish among my friends.

Bruce's turn of phrase gave me pause; that one would go somewhere to be Jewish. As if not being Jewish was even an option. Does the bird sing in order to be a bird? All I knew was that it was inscribed somewhere that I was to be a vertically challenged, wisecracking, and deeply reflective *boychik*.

As I contemplated writing this piece, I observed a pile of stones against a fence in my yard. There lay a tiny piece of cracked concrete, out of which poked a lovely yellow flower. My home abuts a verdant strip along the Rio Fernando. Cottonwoods and box elders, rabbits and magpies, all grace my view. This flower chose the single most unlikely spot from which to sprout.

I could not help but draw the parallel. Rather than rest on the obvious, however, it caused me to further contemplate Bruce's premise. Perhaps he, like most of his cast of characters, came to Taos to find what had evaded them in the moneyed suburbs of New York, Chicago, and L.A. Perhaps they found themselves unknowingly fleeing the rabbinate of the day, which had failed to provide the spiritual sustenance sought by its youth, while simultaneously struggling to provide conclusive dialog around the Holocaust.

Taos is celebrated for so many things: its unique light, its ancient people, its ring of mountains cradling us on all sides; its island-like isolation giving way to endemic twists on language; the church bells by the plaza that toll (for me) as I write; and its sense of community. Taos, not unlike the Jewish experience, is harshness and beauty wrapped in the same cloth.

As a drop of rain does not lose itself when it falls to the sea, so do we retain our stamp in the diaspora. What Taos somehow provided for this band of wandering intellectuals was a spirited ground on which to come together, as Jews. The time and place were ripe, and Bruce and his crew showed up.

Bruce may concede that he found his Yiddishkeit *despite* coming to Taos. But what about tradition, of which we so often speak? Five hundred years ago, we fled Spain for the wilds of this very Rio Grande valley—emphatically, albeit cryptically, to be Jewish. Bruce memorializes a personal continuance of our preternatural wanderings and affirms: This is our portion.

I pose—with humble apology!—that, like the yellow flower emerging from the crack in the concrete, perhaps we did come to Taos to be Jewish.

—Karl Halpert

Introduction

"No one came to Taos to be Jewish" was a phrase I coined in 2002, when the Taos Jewish Center was first formed. It often brings a smile when I say it, maybe because it's so true, or perhaps there is a particularly Jewish ironic twist to it. Whatever it is, I think there is a validity to the idiom.

For years I have wanted to write my impressions of Jewish life in Taos, but I could not find the right form, nor could I decide on the content. Finally, I came up with the notion of writing a combination memoir, biography, and history to include not only my own tale but the story of the Taos rabbis, as well as the Jewish organizations.

I have divided this work into three sections, each with its own particular voice. The first section is my Taos story. Everyone has one of these, and it's often used as an ice breaker: "So what's your Taos story?" and the conversation gets going. In this case, my story is focused on how I came to discover my Jewish heritage right here below Taos Mountain.

The second section is about the three rabbis of Taos: Ron Kalom, Chavah Carp, and Judith HaLevy. Over the past fifty years, other rabbis have come to Taos for periods of time. Some famous ones—like Shlomo Carlebach, Arthur Waskow, and Zalman Schachter-Shalomi—gave workshops at the Lama Foundation or led High Holiday services. (Founded in 1967, Lama is a vibrant spiritual community located north of Taos in the Sangre de Cristo Mountains, perhaps most famous for its association with Ram Dass and printing the original publication of his renowned book *Be Here Now*.) Rabbi Ted Falcon was instrumental in helping form the B'nai Shalom Havurah. Rabbi David Stein and Rabbi Paul Citrin held positions at the Taos Jewish Center, each for several years. And fourteen years ago Rabbi Eli Kaminetzky arrived from Australia by way of New York City and began his term as the head of the Taos Chabad Center. I would respectfully say that if anyone did come to Taos to be Jewish, it would be Rabbi Eli. But in my estimation, Ron Kalom, Chavah Carp, and Judith HaLevy are the only "homegrown" Taos rabbis. The information about the Taos rabbis came primarily from interviews I conducted with each of them in 2011, when I was editor of *HaKol,* the newsletter of the Taos Jewish Center.

In the last section, I chronicle the history of the B'nai Shalom Havurah, the Taos Minyan,* and the Taos

Jewish Center. I also include in this final part a brief history of the Eretz Shalom Cemetery.

As I write this I am somewhat amazed at all that has happened as far as the development of Judaism in the forty-five years I have lived in Taos. I have done my best to write an accurate and inclusive narration of this history. In telling this story from different perspectives, there is some natural reiteration of incidents. As with any historical narrative, there are events, names, and details that might not be included. I hope there will be other writers in the future to fill in the missing pieces that I have unintentionally omitted.

*The quorum required for Jewish communal worship that consists of ten male adults in Orthodox Judaism and usually ten adults of either sex in Conservative and Reform Judaism.

Part 1

Back to the Garden

My Taos Story

Lech Lecha! (Go Forth!)
—Genesis 12:1

No one came to Taos to be Jewish. I certainly did not. In the summer of 1976, my wife Susan and I left Marin County, California, with all our belongings packed into a 1973 Datsun truck. The Golden State had become a bit too golden for us. The taxes, the crowds, and our desire for adventure catapulted us onto the road.

Our dream at the time was to drive cross-country visiting as many wilderness areas and national parks as possible, eventually ending up on the East Coast. From there we planned to store our worldly possessions and travel to Nepal, where we would scale the Himalayas until our wanderlust abated. After that, who knew? We trusted that the next phase of our life would somehow present itself like a rainbow. In fact, in a strange way, it did.

After three months of camping and backpacking, we arrived in Upstate New York, tired and road weary.

Along the way we devoured the North Cascades, the Grand Tetons, Yellowstone, and Glacier National Park, then crossed into Canada and trekked in the Kootenay Range, followed by excursions into Banff and Jasper national parks.

We stopped in Chicago, where I was born, and visited my parents. They had left Chicago in 1952 and moved to Southern California, where I grew up. Then, in 1967, they moved back to Chicago, where my father took a job that furthered his career in the transportation business.

We left Chicago after a couple of days and drove east, exploring the Blue Ridge Mountains, then followed the Appalachian Trail north into Vermont, New Hampshire, and Maine. It was mid-October by the time we settled into the Catskills, where some friends from San Francisco had inherited an old Jewish bungalow colony. The surrounding town was filled with empty kosher butcher shops and abandoned synagogues. The weather in the Northeast had turned cold and dark, so we hunkered down in the cozy little village.

It seemed a bit odd to be in a place that had once bustled with Jews. Where had they all gone? The Catskills had lost their charm. Why go to New Paltz when you could so easily go to Paris or Venice? Whatever the reason, it left us with plenty of space to visit our friends and figure out our next move.

We were tired of traveling and decided we'd wait until the spring to travel to Nepal. Winter in the Catskills was as unappealing as a New York traffic jam. We had the whole country to choose from. Somehow, we managed to save enough money so we didn't have to think about working.

One night I was perusing the *Farmers' Almanac*, looking for sunny places to live, and discovered that Northern New Mexico gets, on average, 300 days a year of sunshine. My eyes drifted to a place named Taos.

I immediately thought of D.H. Lawrence, a favorite writer of mine, and of course the movie *Easy Rider*. But more importantly, it reminded me of a guy named Harvey Mudd, whom I knew from my days as a teacher in San Francisco.

Harvey's daughter was in my class, and he and I got to be a bit chummy. Harvey wrote poetry and lived in Pacific Heights with his wife, Alicia. I recalled several conversations we'd had about Taos. Harvey had a home, maybe a ranch, there, and my recollection was that he had plenty of room and knew everyone in town. If I were ever there, he'd said, I should look him up, because he was moving back.

My wife liked the idea. Taos sounded like an intriguing and romantic place, and between the sun, the mountains, and the skiing, it might be the perfect place to winter.

The next day we loaded the truck and headed west. Nepal would still be there come April. We arrived in late October. Everything brimmed with golden light: the aspens, the mountains, the sky. The air was crisp with the smell of apples and piñon fires. To say it was magical those first days doesn't nearly describe the ambiance of the place. I had grown up in the suburban tract confines of the San Fernando Valley in Southern California. Nothing in that experience prepared me for this high mesa with its adobe homes, cottonwood trees, and the looming Sangre de Cristo Mountains. For a guy in search of natural wonders, open space, and a refuge from a middle-class acquisitive culture, Taos was about as far away as you could get without crossing a national border.

I never found Harvey Mudd; he had moved to Santa Fe. But I did connect with his best friend Jim Levy. Susan and I wound up spending our first few months in Taos in a little adobe outbuilding powered by an electric cord running from his house.

The Levy home was situated on a shelf above the Rio Hondo, and for Susan and me, it was like a glorified camping experience. We hit it off with Jim and his wife, Phaedra Greenwood, right from the start. They were and still are both writers, and, as it turned out, Jim had grown up in Southern California, so we had plenty to share. Of course, neither Jim nor I came to Taos to be

Jewish, but nevertheless, Jim would later play a significant role in the formation of the Taos Jewish Center.

In the fall of 1976, we did not have a clue that anything Jewish was in our future. Far from it, Jim and I were more interested in sharing our interests in D.H. Lawrence, frolicking in the Rio Grande, and absorbing the fall colors of the Taos Valley.

Susan and I never made it to Nepal. After our first winter in Taos, we decided to try again, but this time we figured we'd leave from San Francisco. While in the Bay Area, we changed our minds about which great mountain range we wanted to explore and decided on the Andes instead of the Himalayas. There were several reasons.

By now we were both smitten with Taos as our home base, and we thought traveling through Central and South America would give us the opportunity to learn Spanish, which was going to come in handy living in Taos, where the majority of the residents were Hispanic. The Andes also appealed to us because they were more accessible and wouldn't require a lot of technical climbing to reach the higher peaks.

Susan and I spent four months traveling and trekking between Mexico and Ecuador and finished the trip with a three-week adventure in the Galapagos. Our traveling itch had been sufficiently scratched, and we decided it was time to settle down and make a home in Taos. In 1978, we bought a small cabin on the banks of the Rio Hondo, just downstream from Jim and Phaedra.

Nothing Jewish was happening in Taos, except our immediate neighbor was a Jewish man named Larry Taub, a lawyer and accountant from the East Coast. I soon found myself playing pickup basketball games with Ted Dimond, a Jewish guy from New York. Shortly thereafter, I became friends with Cid Backer, another New York Jew, who was driving a bread delivery truck for a bakery called Workingman's Bread, located in El Prado next to the Amigos Co-op.

Basketball definitely became my connection to the world of Taos Judaism, because it was also where I met Roger Lerman, who would later become not only my Torah study partner but a leader in many future Taos Jewish projects. Roger was a tough power forward who had an uncanny way of blocking my way to the basket and always had a hearty laugh as he stumbled over my banged-up body. Ted, Roger, Cid, and Jim would become lifelong friends.

After basketball games we sometimes adjourned to the House of Taos, where another Jew, Ron Kalom, made the best pizzas in town. Kalom, like me, was born in Chicago. But whereas I left at the age of five for California, Ron stayed and got his education at Francis Parker School and later graduated from Roosevelt University.

Ron didn't play basketball; he worked and played on the stage at the Taos Community Auditorium. A consummate actor, perhaps his most renowned role was as Tevye in *Fiddler on the Roof*. He was a natural for the part, being tall, lean, and sporting a full bushy beard. Ron had the voice, the temperament, and chutzpah for the role.

If he wasn't already known as "The Taos Jew," because he was the only person in Taos who regularly wore a *kippa*, he certainly became The Taos Jew after the production of *Fiddler*. Little did I know, back in the early House of Taos days, how much of an influence he would have on my Jewish life.

I should note that the director of *Fiddler* was a New Jersey transplant by the name of Judith Fritz. She, too, would have a dynamic influence on Jewish life in Taos when she became Rabbi Judith HaLevy.

In June of 1980, my first son was born—without doubt, one of the most profound and joyous days of my life. So now I had a son, a Jewish son, and of course I had to find someone to perform a *brit milah*—a Jewish circumcision. I didn't come to Taos to be Jewish, yet I was faced with my first real act of being a Jew in a new land.

As fate, or as God, would have it, my next-door neighbor, Larry Taub, had moved into town and rented his house to a Jewish doctor. Ken Brandis was a family physician as well as a member of our local pickup basketball team. After one of our games, I asked him, "By the way, do you do circumcisions?" Strange question, but there we were—two Jews sitting around trying to catch our breath; he was a doctor and I was the father of a newborn Jewish boy.

"Sure," he said.

"Well, what about some prayers to go along with the snip?" I asked.

"I'm not a *mohel*," he said, "but I think between the two of us we can figure something out." We did.

By the time my second son was born, Dr. Brandis had moved; yet miraculously, I had befriended two more Jewish doctors, Jack and Pat Nobel. Pat was our pediatrician, and her husband, Jack, a surgeon, had performed plenty of circumcisions. The Taos medical landscape then and now was not without its share of Jews. Doctors Schreiber, Rosen, and Kaufman tended to the ailing Taos populace. Later, Doctors Guttmann, Lubowitz, and Reich added to the ranks.

I didn't come to Taos to be Jewish, but somehow I had managed to surround myself with Jewish friends, a Jewish doctor, and now I had *two* Jewish sons. Family life unfolded as it does with all its necessities, celebrations, and of course, holidays.

My parents had practiced a relaxed form of Conservative Judaism, so I was familiar with traditional observances, although after I went off to college, I discarded them as unnecessary for the kind of life I wanted to live. I imagined myself as a kind of free spirit that hearkened more to the wisdom of Thoreau, Emerson, and Aldo Leopold than to the precepts of the Torah. I also had an interest in Eastern philosophies that had been predigested by American writers like Alan Watts and the poet Gary Snyder. That kind of outlook on the world fit right in with the wave of hippie types who had been coming to Taos in the '60s and '70s.

Before long my first son, Teo, started asking questions about Christmas and Easter. After all, we lived in a small Catholic community, and Easter-egg hunts and Christmas trees abounded during those seasons. For a while, my wife and I indulged those amusements and partook in a very limited way. By the time Teo was two or three, I knew he had to have some kind of education and understanding about his heritage. I remember him asking me, "What am I?"

"What do you mean?" I said.

"The kids at school want to know what I am."

Whatever umbrage I might have taken with Judaism at the time melted away when I realized I needed to answer the existential query that my son had put to me. I had no right to deny him his identity or his heritage. The Christmas tree gave way to a homemade menorah. He and I went into the forest and found a stout oak branch about three inches in diameter. It had a lovely curve to it and was about fourteen inches long, just enough space to drill nine holes to hold the candles for Hanukkah. It had been a long time, but I had not forgotten my mother's recipe for potato latkes, so the torch began to be passed from one generation to the next via candles, dreidels, and latkes.

While living in Arroyo Hondo in the late '70s, I met Grove Burnett, an environmental lawyer who represented a small organization called the Committee to Save the Rio Hondo. At the time, we were involved in a lawsuit against the Taos Ski Valley for polluting the river out my back door.

Grove and I became friendly over the years, and one winter, he invited me to go on a cross-country ski trip to his Vallecito Retreat Center. It was a twelve-mile trek to the lodge, and when we arrived I met a young man from somewhere in Asia—India or Nepal; I don't recall exactly where. Grove had become interested in Vipassana meditation and used the center to host both spiritual and environmental retreats. The young fellow who greeted us was both the caretaker and a devotee of Vipassana meditation. For whatever reason, we took an immediate liking to each other and were soon discussing the ills of the world.

My interest in Eastern philosophy led me to read more and more books about Buddhism, and I continued to find it curious that so many of the writers and disciples of Buddhism had Jewish names: Stephen Levine, Sylvia Borstein, Richard Alpert (Ram Dass), Bernard Glassman, Sharon Salzberg, Joseph Goldstein, Jack Kornfield, and many others. The famous Renewal Rabbi, Zalman Schachter-Shalomi, made a deep connection with the Dalai Lama that was chronicled in Rodger Kamenetz's famous book *The Jew in the Lotus*. A new term, JewBu, had been coined to describe this spiritual hybrid. I researched the early lives of each of these teachers and invariably found that they had all been raised Jewish. What happened?

My newly acquired Buddhist friend offered me tea after I got my pack off and had squared away my belongings. As we sipped aromatic jasmine tea, he asked, "So what is your practice?" At first, I had no idea what he was asking. Practice? Like my tennis serve or my job? He saw my bewilderment and smiled gently. "Your spiritual practice, I mean." Of course, I thought, after all, I'm at a retreat center and this young guy is probably a monk in training. But what *was* my practice?

Without another I thought, I said, "I'm a Jew."

"Oh how wonderful. A very noble path," he said.

"Well, I suppose," I said. "But I never thought about it as a *practice*."

A wall of comfortable silence rested between us as we sipped our tea. Out of nowhere I decided to ask him if he had any insight into why so many Jews had fled Judaism to become teachers and even masters of Buddhist teaching. Without hesitation, he floored me with a keen discourse about the Holocaust. He began:

> The rabbis had failed to find a way to address the unbearable grief that resulted in such a horrific loss. Many of your brightest and most compassionate teachers and leaders drifted away because they couldn't find a pathway to handle the profound sorrow and deep emotions that arose from that tragic event. Buddhist practice inculcates a way to engage our difficult feelings and thoughts through empathy and acceptance. It wasn't so much that the rabbis did any wrong. They just were not prepared, and I think there was also a great deal of shame that they could not transform.

His response stunned me. Whether it reflected the truth or his solo riff on the post-Holocaust world, I still do not know. But what he said certainly made sense in the context of my Jewish education, or lack thereof. It had no historical or spiritual relevance for me. As far as the Holocaust and my response or reaction, all I recalled was silence and an occasional *Kaddish* prayer during the High Holidays, as if it were just an afterthought to an already too long liturgy. How do we reconcile and find some kind of redemptive response to an epic catastrophe? For the Buddhists, you sit, you dwell, and you observe the vicissitudes of the mind and confounding tragedy that rifles through your consciousness until you find peace. I'd never learned how to accomplish that.

Yet my Jewish connections continued to grow seamlessly. Soon there was another Jewish boy in the neighborhood, Mathew Rutherford, the son of Wayne Rutherford and Rose Gordon. Matt, Teo, and Cid and Betty Backer's two sons, Lee and Kellan, became close friends, and our families hung out together quite a bit.

I'm not sure how it happened that we heard about a Jewish Sunday school run by Carol Carp, but we did. It was 1986 or 1987. Carol would later be ordained as Rabbi Chavah Carp. At the time she was running the school out of her home in Ranchos de Taos. We signed the boys up and, for a while, they enjoyed it. But soon soccer and taekwondo took over, and the children lost interest.

Nonetheless, the experience broadened my sense of the Taos Jewish community. There was more here than I had imagined, but I still wasn't so keen about getting involved, nor did Jewish studies interest me that much. What I was doing regarding Judaism was strictly for the kids. At the time I was running the Taos Valley School, a private school with pre-K through eighth grade, and I had little time for other distractions.

All that changed one Sunday afternoon when I was watching a movie with my boys, *The Outside Chance of Maximilian Glick*, about two adolescents—a girl and a boy—who were both piano prodigies. He was Jewish and she was Catholic, and his family wasn't happy about them getting so close, so they finagled a way to separate them. There was a scene about the boy's bar mitzvah.

After the movie, Teo asked me if he could do that.
"Do what?" I asked. "Learn to play the piano?"
"No. Have a bar mitzvah."
I was floored but didn't show it. "Of course you can have a bar mitzvah, if that's what you want."

Meanwhile, I recalled a vow I had made shortly after my own bar mitzvah, which was an excruciating event in my life. I'd never, ever force my kid into going through that process unless *he wanted it*. My bar mitzvah preparation took two and a half years, and it consisted of weekly afternoon classes the first year and half, and then twice a week for the last year. The worst part of the ordeal was I had no perspective for the process. No, the worst part was that none of my friends were in the academy I attended. No, the worst part was that I missed Little League practice. No, the worst part was that it was a half-hour drive each way through San Fernando Valley traffic, and I was stuck in the car with a group of kids who were weird, and the only thing we had in common was the archaic Valley Hebrew Academy.

That whining track of my thirteen-year-old self played through my noggin as my sweet little ten-year-old innocently asked me about a bar mitzvah. I suppose my experience wasn't so much traumatic as it was one of alienating me from Judaism. It offered me no context or relevancy with what was happening in my world of the late '50s and early '60s.

I wasn't alone. It seemed like all my friends had lost touch with the tradition for one reason or another. Judaism existed in Taos, but there wasn't anything of interest for me.

Regardless, I needed to find a way to make my son a bar mitzvah. Through the Jewish grapevine, I knew that Ron Kalom, on occasion, prepared boys for that ritual. I knew that Larry Schreiber's son Lucas and Judith Fritz's son Eliam had studied with Ron. So I made the call and popped the question. "Would you consider preparing Teo to become a bar mitzvah?" There was a pause at the other end of the line. Finally, he started to speak.

"Well, it's not so simple as just preparing Teo. I need to talk with you, Susan, and Teo and make sure you are ready."

Later that week, Ron came over for dinner and we talked. And we talked. And we talked. Ron was a delight. He stressed the importance of support, involvement, and the calendar. The calendar? Judaism is based on a particular cycle of events, holidays, and festivals, he elucidated. Preparation for a young person needs to have a framework, needs to be integrated and relevant. Oh, now I was realizing for the first time that there was someone in Taos, unlike me, who had found a significant way to connect to Judaism. Most importantly, he went on, you'll need to do something to observe the Sabbath; otherwise everything I teach him will just be an abstraction, and it will be a waste of time for all of us.

I looked around the table and asked for feedback from my son and wife. They were both all in, so we began the journey. Teo started meeting weekly with Ron. We started lighting candles on Friday night; and, as we had already been doing during Passover, we held a family *seder*—often inviting friends like the Backers.

After a few months of observing Teo's interest in working with Ron, I felt a longing to get deeper into the journey myself. I knew that Roger Lerman had also taken an interest in renewing his connection to Judaism. Roger had started a practice of studying the weekly Torah portion. Sometimes Judith Fritz, who was studying to become a rabbi, joined him. Every so often, after our basketball games, Roger invited me to join him on Saturday afternoon for Torah study.

It had never appealed to me until now. If my son was going to learn the basics of Jewish knowledge, I would join him. I called Roger and asked if the Torah offer was still on, and he said, "Absolutely." And so began a long relationship in Jewish theology and philosophy with Roger. Our basketball battles turned into Torah wrestling on a weekly basis. Our friendship built a pathway that led to many other aspects of Jewish life in Taos. Another friend, Bruce Ross, and I also decided to join together and engage in Torah study with Ron. We met on Saturdays for a year or more, while Teo prepared with Ron.

In 1988, my close friend Ted Dimond, at age 35, decided that he wanted to learn more about his Jewish heritage. One afternoon, while pushing his two young children on the swing set at Enos Garcia Elementary School, Ron, who lived in the neighborhood, strolled through the playground. Ted had known Ron from the local radio station, KXRT (later it became KTAO), where they both had radio programs. The conversation about learning more about Judaism transformed into the idea of becoming a bar mitzvah. Ted had been raised in a secular home, and the idea of bar mitzvah never occurred to him or his family. In 1991, at age 38,

Ted Dimond became a bar mitzvah and continued his studies with Ron.

When the High Holidays arrived, Bruce, Ted, Ron, and I all gathered on the Kaloms' large deck overlooking Sunset Park off Valverde Street, directly across from the Taos Public Library. In our bare feet, we stood and *davened* (prayed) through the entire service, stopping only to drink water and take a bathroom break. With Taos Mountain looming to the north, Tres Piedras dancing in the west, and the fall air invigorating our lungs, it was one of the most memorable Jewish experiences of my life. Four guys, four tones, four souls all leaning into the ineffable and inspiring light of the southern Rocky Mountains. It was an audacious reckoning with an ancient tradition. Suddenly I felt the spiritual freedom and authenticity that had eluded me all my life.

Teo's bar mitzvah took place on June 12, 1993, one day after his thirteenth birthday, at the Mabel Dodge Luhan House. At the time, the historic site was owned by George and Kitty Otero. They used it as a place to conduct educational workshops, and had recently added a large multi-use space that they rented out for special events. The Mabel Dodge House was built in 1918 by Tony Lujan for his wife, the wealthy art and literary salon queen Mabel Dodge. It became a creative gathering place for the likes of D.H. Lawrence, Alfred

Stieglitz, Georgia O'Keeffe, Willa Cather, and others. In 1970, Dennis Hopper bought it while filming *Easy Rider* and turned it into a local artist collective.

The rite of passage was a joyous affair. Ron Kalom held the room with tremendous gravitas and gave it a kind of spiritual eloquence, transcending time and space, yet the entire affair was as comfortable as a family gathering around the living room hearth. After the service and the food, I found myself in an intimate circle of friends: Ron Kalom, Roger Lerman, Ted Dimond, and Bruce Ross. While munching on *rugelach* that my mother had made and brought from Chicago, we all confessed that there was a mutual feeling of sorrow about the ending of our individual studies now that the bar mitzvah was over.

Ron acknowledged this as well, but then he said, "Well, we don't have to stop. We can form a *minyan* and meet together. I think we can do that." We all looked at each in bewilderment. A minyan? The discussion continued, and we all decided we would give it a try. We would meet at Ted Dimond's house in two weeks. That would give us time to gather our thoughts and see if there were any others who would like to join us.

Those years between 1993 and 2002 were filled with awe and inspiration. After the first few years, I realized that, for the first time in my life, I had uncovered a real connection with my tradition. This was primarily because Ron Kalom revealed sources that I never knew existed in terms of philosophy and theology. Thanks to him, the study of Torah became an open-ended journey into the minds of many of the world's great thinkers and, more importantly, into a realm of profound existential questions, like the nature of good and evil and the meaning of suffering. Together, he and I plowed through the Book of Job and, with a few others, diligently read Leon Wieseltier's stellar book on grief, *Kaddish*.

One of the great philosophers and theologians of the twentieth century was Rabbi Abraham Joshua Heschel. He walked arm in arm with Martin Luther King in Selma, Alabama. In all my years of Jewish learning up to the time of the minyan, I had never heard his name mentioned. Ron had been reading him for years, and soon my library was filled with Heschel's books; but more important, soon my head was filled with Heschel's words, ideas, poetry, and theological concepts, such as *Man is not alone in the world. Just as man is in search of God, God is in search for man.*

Suddenly Judaism wasn't an abstraction or obligation; it was an authentic relationship. As Martin Buber called it, an "I-Thou" connection. It was a conversation. It was a wrestle and a search, and I had partners in this quest. Why do we have a consciousness that can appreciate the concept of awe? How and why do we seek to create holiness? What does it mean to create a cathedral in time? Heschel's questions got me fully engaged in my relationship with Judaism. And it wasn't just Heschel. No, it was a whole busload of writers and thinkers: Martin Buber, Adin Steinsaltz, Rabbi Joseph Soloveitchik, Gershom Scholem, Emil Fackenheim, and of course, Elie Wiesel. Before long, I had my own Jewish library that now contains hundreds of volumes. Beyond the philosophers and rabbis, there was the great heft of Jewish writers that found their way into our morning service: Phillip Roth, Franz Kafka, Robert Pinsky, Bernard Malamud, Cynthia Ozick, Issac Bashevis Singer, Marge Piercy, as well as more contemporary authors, such as Jonathan Safran Foer, Nicole Krauss, and Michael Chabon. Ron found a way to integrate literature into our weekly Torah study. And there was always *The New Yorker* magazine. For as many times as David Remnick was quoted, he could have been an honorary member of the minyan.

My entire adult life I'd had an approach/avoidance relationship with Israel. At times, I felt fiercely protective and dedicated to the tiny homeland of my heritage, most especially after the '67 and '73 wars; at other times I experienced shame and anger toward the right-wing policies that targeted the Palestinian people and looked more and more like apartheid. Some years, I had felt an almost sacred desire to reunite with the country of my descendants, and there were also times when I thought it was the last place on earth I wanted to be.

Finally, in the spring of 1995, the time had arrived. My appetite for a closer, more intimate, understanding of the place where all the myths and history began was aroused. Politically, the climate was relatively mellow—at least for Israel—and I kept thinking about Rabbi Hillel's adage, "If not now, when?" My initial hope was for the entire family to go for a couple months. I was ready to put my life on hold and have the once-in-a-lifetime experience. But Susan wasn't prepared to take the plunge, and without her, I wasn't going to take the children.

So it would be a solo journey into the promised land, and that was fine with me. A week or two passed, and I thought again about traveling alone and wondered if perhaps my friend Bruce Ross might want to travel with me. We were close, and having a companion would not only be safer, but I'd have someone to share the experience with. If he said no, it wasn't going to change anything. I was going.

Bruce jumped at the invitation. I had already done a lot of research and spoken with Roger Lerman, who had lived in Israel for a good deal of time. Roger's information was invaluable. Not only did he connect me with a perfect place to stay in Jerusalem, the St Andrews Scottish Guest House located adjacent to the

Old City, but he also put us in touch with his close friend Gabriel Levin, a poet and literary maven who turned out to be a great human being, as well as one connected with the Israeli and Palestinian writers' community. Gabriel is renowned in his own right as a poet and is the son of the famous Israeli writer and scholar Meyer Levin, who twice won the National Jewish Book Award and is the author of *An Israel Haggadah for Passover*, which we used every year at the Lerman Passover *seder*.

The Scottish guesthouse, located across from the Valley of Hinnom, looking out to the Jaffa Gate in the Old City of Jerusalem, offered a complete counterpoint to the deep Jewish atmosphere of Israel. Administered by a Scottish church group and employing mostly Palestinians, it gave us a genuine connection to both peoples who lived in the sacred city. I quickly became friends with one of the managers, Emma, and in addition to Gabriel Levin, she became one of our guides through the city.

Before leaving for Israel, I had arranged two trips outside the country. One into the Egyptian Sinai with the Society for the Preservation of Nature in Israel, and the other across the recently opened Jordanian border to the hidden city of Petra. The Sinai trip consisted of backpacking and camping in the high mountains of the Sinai, the legendary landscape where Moses and the Hebrews had their epic meeting and, according to the Torah, received the Ten Commandments.

Our secular wilderness guide, when asked about the particular site, replied, "I don't believe in fairy tales. You can believe whatever you want, but any of these mountains could be called Mount Sinai. Take your choice." We had two Bedouin guides leading the way with their camels, who were carrying most of our gear. The nights were as cold as the days were warm, and I slept soundly under the purest desert sky I had ever seen. At least I knew that if there really were such a person as Moses, he would have seen the same sky that I now witnessed. That was enough for me.

Petra, oh beautiful ancient Nabataean wonderland! It's called the Red Rose City for the extraordinary crimson color of the stone. We crossed the border between Israel and Jordon by walking through a 100-yard stretch of no-man's-land. There were no signs or instructions after we cleared the Israeli side. We were told we'd know what to do once we got on the other side. Bruce and I quickly moved through an immigration kiosk and found a long line of ancient Mercedes Benz taxis ready to ferry us into the never-never land of Petra. As we sped through the biblical landscape, our driver pointed out several camel caravans trekking across the desert. The only thing separating us from the ancient world of Canaan was a 1964 German-made automobile.

We were a long, long way from Taos. My newly discovered interest in Judaism thrust me back in time, and my imagination catapulted through the portions of the Torah where Jews were wandering in the wilderness. Not only Jews, but the ancient Nabataeans roamed this place between the fourth and second centuries BCE.

Like in so many places across Asia, Europe, and Africa, the Romans left their indelible seal, their genius for architecture, and their iron hand of power and conquest. Nothing symbolized all of that more profoundly than Al-Khazneh, the Roman Treasury ruin in the center of Petra, made famous in the Hollywood blockbuster *Indiana Jones and the Last Crusade*. The monument is as graceful and beautiful as any building on earth. The reality that it has remained intact since the first century makes it a true wonder of the world. I didn't come to Taos to be Jewish, and I certainly never in my life imagined I would be standing in the middle of an ancient Roman kingdom as part of a trip to the Holy Land.

More than the thrill and amazement of Petra, there was also an intimate and familial aspect of my journey. A few years before my mother passed away, I was introduced to my cousins from Israel during a short visit to Las Vegas, Nevada, where my parents had retired. At the time, I thought nothing of it. The cousins were probably in their late sixties. Shoshana was my mother's first cousin, but they had only met once during another visit to the United States. Both Shoshana's parents, my grandmother's sister and her husband, and all Shoshana's relatives who remained in Poland were massacred by the Nazis at the beginning of the war. Shoshana and her sister survived by hiding in the forest until they met a brave, kindhearted farmer who hid them in his barn. After the war, she and her sister immigrated to Israel and married men who were officers in the Haganah during the 1948 Arab-Israeli war.

When I decided to go to Israel, I contacted Shoshana and her husband, Reuben. They invited me to stay with them in Petah Tikva (Gateway of Hope in Hebrew), a small suburb north of Tel Aviv, and suggested that I spend the Passover holiday with them.

A family in Israel? Survivors of the Holocaust? Any incredulity that might have remained about my Judaism vanished as I sat among my Israeli family and celebrated the feast of the *matzos* with them. They were a jovial group, as full of questions as I was.

The day after the *seder*, Reuben and his brother-in-law Samuel took me on a history tour of the land north and east of Petah Tikva. They wanted me to see the places where they had made a stand during the war. They wanted me to walk the revered ground where recent and ancient blood had been spilled in order to preserve their hallowed country. They drove me to the town of Modi'in, famous for being the birthplace of the Maccabees, whose exploits are rekindled every year at Hanukkah. It was in this same hill country, southeast of Tel Aviv, that my two relatives led a valiant counterattack against the invading Syrian and Jordanian armies. History repeats itself over and over again in this part of the world.

Three months later I returned home, feeling that a transformation had taken place. A piece of my life now included a geographic sanctification; it felt like a cellular puzzle had been resolved within me. I had walked the land of my ancestors. I brought that vitality into the minyan and plumbed the texts with newfound enthusiasm. The biblical commentaries deconstructing the original words of Torah now had a more visceral meaning. I had hiked the Sinai and had prayed beneath the Temple Mount.

Of course, the rest of my life moved forward as well. Not long after I returned, my mother died. It rocked my world. For the first time I really understood the meaning and purpose of the *Kaddish*. The prayer became my container for the grief I was experiencing. I used it as a way to define the boundaries of my anguish, and the minyan provided the communal space and support for my loss.

Shortly after my mother died, in 1996, my younger son, Robin, started studying with Ron. Robin never asked about his bar mitzvah; he knew from observing his older brother that he would follow in his footsteps. Over the years, he and Ron had already bonded, so his transition into the process was smooth. During the time Teo had studied with Ron, Robin often attended the minyan service. Now it was Robin's turn to sit with us from time to time. I felt tremendous gratitude for what Ron and the minyan were providing.

In 1997, Susan and I separated and later divorced. The disintegration of our family was devastating for all of us. A fissure had been growing for some time, but I had hoped it wouldn't split before the children left home. It didn't happen that way. Teo was about to graduate from high school and move on to college. Robin was in middle school and grounded in sports. He also had Ron every week, and I know that helped during the transition. My weekly meetings with the minyan and my connection with Judaism kept me focused and brought me great comfort during my new life as a single man and a single parent. The next couple of years whizzed by. As Robin's bar mitzvah approached, in May of 1999, my life had become fuller than it had ever been. Busy with work, busy with Robin's life as a soccer dad and supporting his bar mitzvah study, busy with my social life, and busy with writing in my spare time. Life was good.

Robin had a beautiful bar mitzvah at the San Geronimo Lodge. All the members of the minyan attended, along with my friends and relatives, as well as Susan's. It was a large ceremony with great food, music, and dancing. I didn't come to Taos to be Jewish, yet everyone who attended the festivities recognized that Judaism was truly flourishing in the Taos Valley. What could be more Jewish than a gala celebration like this? And still I wondered what would be next.

I loved being single. After twenty-six years with the same woman, I found it liberating and fascinating to be on my own. I diligently covered all my parental and financial responsibilities. My inner community consisted of lifelong friends, a men's support group, and of course, the minyan. The minyan was the anchor. Regardless of anything else, I knew that every Saturday for fifty-two weeks we would be meeting, praying, and studying. I prepared each week, often writing notes and crafting my own personal commentary on the weekly portion. One year I decided to write a poem about each Torah chapter. The whole experience filled me, and I did not want.

One of our minyan members, Carmi Plaut, was getting married in the fall of 1999. Carmi had recently moved here from Chicago and came from a family of Reform rabbis. Both his father and his brother Josh were rabbis. His uncle, Gunther Plaut, was a famous scholar and rabbi in the Jewish Reform movement and was the editor of the big red book found in most

Reform synagogues, *The Torah: A Modern Commentary*. The book was published by the Union of American Hebrew Congregations. Another major contributor to the work was Professor William Hallo of Yale University. Coincidentally, both Gunther Plaut and William Hallo had been on the faculty of the Hebrew Union College in Cincinnati when Ron Kalom was attending. Carmi's presence in the minyan added a great deal, and he would be instrumental in helping found the Taos Jewish Center. On a more personal note, he was also indirectly responsible for my meeting the love of my life.

On Friday night, before Carmi's wedding, there was a Shabbat gathering at the Martinez Hacienda on Ranchitos Road, located right next to Roger and Roberta Lerman's home. Everything felt interconnected; one thing led to the next; one person knew someone from another person's hometown. Things were happening fast.

As I mentioned, I was single during this period and had just driven into the parking lot, where I met up with Roger Lerman and Bruce Ross, when I noticed a pretty woman with exquisite curly golden hair pull into the driveway in a white Saab convertible. She exited her car and started to look around, slightly bewildered since there was no sign or even an obvious entrance to the hacienda. There was a little footbridge that separated the two parts of the parking lot, and I walked over and asked the attractive blond if she was looking for the pre-wedding Shabbat. She was. We introduced ourselves. Her name was Cindy Sadow. I offered to show her the way, and together we crossed over the bridge.

It turned out that Cindy had attended the minyan the previous week, while I was away. That's how she had found out about the celebration. She was very excited because it turned out that Joshua Plaut, who was leading the service and was going to perform the wedding, was also the rabbi on Martha's Vineyard, where Cindy's sister Jacqui lived, whom Josh knew. Cindy and I talked and talked throughout the evening, and while neither of us acknowledged it at the time, something special had sparked.

Although both Cindy and I were seeing other people at the time, our friendship through the minyan grew more interesting and compelling. Usually, after the service ended, she and Bruce Ross and I adjourned to the The Bean, a sweet little café that was owned by another old friend, Peter Miceli. Our conversation from the minyan table moved to a table at The Bean, with great coffee and delicious Southwestern eggs. But more than the food, Cindy's and my connection became warm and familiar, as if we had known each other our entire lives. I didn't come to Taos to be Jewish, nor was I in Taos seeking a Jewish partner, but things kept rolling along. As the chapters of the Torah unfurled week after week, she and I kept the conversation going, sometimes by phone or, occasionally, we got together for drinks or a walk.

When New Year's Eve 2000 came along, I decided to have a party, mostly with friends from the minyan. Interestingly, even though Cindy and I were otherwise romantically occupied, both of us were without dates that night. I invited her and asked her to bring her guitar. By now it was no secret that she had a gorgeous voice and a repertoire that ranged from Judy Collins songs to Jewish standards like "My Yiddishe Mama." The party was a tremendous success, and when the historic hour arrived, I found myself standing outside, alone with Cindy, saying hello to a new century.

Not long after that, I took a winter vacation in Hawaii. While I was there, Cindy, who had come to Taos not to be Jewish but to ski, had an awful ski accident. She literally fell off the mountain. Fortunately, other than being terrified and having some nasty lacerations, she survived without any broken bones. By the time I got back to the minyan, she was back as well. We renewed our friendship and continued our regular after-minyan lunches.

There had been a long history of community *seders* in Taos, dating back to the '60s. In 1974, Ron

Kalom drafted a *Haggadah* that he called "The Westside Haggadah," because he lived on the west side of the plaza. Having come from Chicago, Ron had a propensity for defining things geographically, as was done in the city. With the new century upon us, the minyan decided we would conduct a large community *seder* at the San Geronimo Lodge. "The Westside Haggadah" hadn't been revised in over a decade, and for reasons that are still too mysterious for me to completely comprehend, Cindy and I volunteered to revise a new version. The word *Haggadah* means tale or story, and the creation of the new *Haggadah* became our story.

During February, March, and April of 2000, Cindy and I sat hip to hip in front of my old Gateway computer in my tiny home office. The revision work went slowly. Cindy was a meticulous editor, and I loved doing research into the reasons for the prayers, as well as looking for contemporary commentaries. We got together once or twice a week. Something started to click between the *maggid* and the blessing over the *matzo*. How could this be? Week after week I sat with a Jewish woman from New Jersey, rewriting the traditional Jewish story, here in Taos, New Mexico. For someone who didn't come to Taos to be Jewish, I found myself in a thicket of Jewish reeds while rewriting the Exodus story, and somehow knew I was heading toward my own promised land. "The Westside Passover Haggadah" had morphed into a love story. Several times after our work sessions, we climbed a ladder to my roof and shared glasses of iced vodka while gazing at the stars and the moon. We both knew something was happening, although our dedication to the *Haggadah* project kept us on track, at least for a while.

On April 21, 2000, we all gathered at the San Geronimo Lodge and prepared for a large *seder* filled with music, frivolity, and a newly revised "Passover Haggadah." Before we got started, someone started howling outside. *Come out! Come out!* Everyone ran outside to witness a blessing—the most astonishing sunset anyone had ever seen. That is saying a lot considering the exquisite sunsets that abound in the Taos Valley. We were stunned into silence as the sun melted into the horizon of Tres Piedras; the sky lit up into a flurry of purples, reds, and yellows, all melting and dancing into a slow waltz, then lingering in a silent symphony. A heralding of extraordinary significance, this would be a special Passover for everyone, especially Cindy and me. The entire event was a great success and a validation for the minyan. There were more than seventy people in attendance, and the revised *Haggadah* was appreciated by all.

When Passover ended, Cindy and I realized that what we had together was more than just a friendship. Our shared time in the minyan, our long talks over lunch, and the experience with the *Haggadah* deepened our relationship. Soon we were hiking together, backpacking, and taking long vacations to exquisite places, like the Island of Bequia in the Grenadines. The time together flowed seamlessly, but I still wasn't sure if I was ready to get married again.

My cousin Judy's youngest son, Warren, was having a bar mitzvah in San Diego. Out of the blue, I decided I'd ask Cindy if she wanted to join me, thinking all the while that the last thing she'd be interested in doing was going to a bar mitzvah. Boy, was I wrong. Without a second's hesitation she said, "I'd love it." Not only did I not come to Taos to be Jewish, I certainly never imagined I'd meet a woman who loved going to Jewish celebrations! Cindy met my extended family, and my uncles, in particular, were wowed by her. My Uncle Martin, my father's youngest brother, gave me a wink and a big thumbs up as he pointed with his thick chin toward Cindy. Our relationship blossomed and came to fruition on May 24, 2002, when we were married by Rabbi Joe Black at Congregation Albert in Albuquerque. Rabbi Black was a colleague of Josh Plaut, as well as a friend of Carmi Plaut. Cindy had known Joe from when she lived in Albuquerque and was part of the congregation.

The minyan had nurtured me in more ways than there are letters in the Jewish alphabet. I felt sated spiritually, and my life was very full. Later, I was guiding the Taos Jewish Center on its inaugural cruise. How all this had transpired compelled me to once again check my Jewish radar screen.

My belief in a Jewish God still didn't exactly make sense to me. Being a Jew was one thing. I had no doubt that I was a member of a historical people, a large tribe with a rich and well-documented history, and that reality resonated deep in my core. But all the study and prayer still didn't answer the universal questions about a supreme being and its connection to a source named *Hashem*. What in the world was I doing heading up the TJC anyway? One part of me felt thrust forward with the force of a speedboat on full throttle, and another part questioned my agency in taking on such a task. And where was God in any of this? Maybe in the energy, maybe in the will to make choices, maybe in the synchronicity of all that had happened in the last twenty years, and maybe just in my wondering about all of it. Like Einstein and Spinoza, I do not believe in an anthropomorphic male deity with long white whiskers flying through clouds casting down plagues and sending out angels do his bidding. What I witness when I gaze into the Taos night is the silky haze of the milky way and all the galaxies beyond. The existence of life and of the universe is a profound mystery beyond my understanding. Certainly, there is order and there is beauty. Like Einstein said, "We see the universe marvelously arranged and obeying certain laws but only dimly understand these laws. Our limited minds grasp the mysterious force that moves the constellations." As Carl Sagan, another famous Jew-non-Jew scientist, once said, "We are all stardust." Joni Mitchell echoed the same notion in the song "Woodstock."

We are stardust
We are golden
And we've got to get ourselves
Back to the garden…

In my *religious* brain, that translates to the fact we are all part of creation, and our creator is part of us. The rest of the story is just our individual commentaries. Yet in a strange cosmic fashion, for many of us coming to Taos was like "getting ourselves back to the garden."

My thoughts at the time of inception of the Taos Jewish Center were that it was important to have a place where people could wrestle with their own personal issues regarding what it meant to be a Jew in Taos, New Mexico. For whatever reason, that was and still is important to me. Taos is a peculiar place in its own way; being a Jew in this wilderness is even more odd and isolating. Yet somehow, my Jewish experience unfurled as naturally as the snow that falls on Taos Mountain every winter.

As I reflect back after almost thirty years of involvement with Judaism in Taos, it is nothing less than remarkable. My good fortune is that I found a wise and inspiring teacher who also became a beloved friend. I discovered a road map into the intricacies of the Torah with a facility that allows me to delve, challenge, research, and mostly appreciate the ancient writing of my ancestors, the *people of the book*. The engagement is a lifelong process that provides comfort, stimulation, and awe. Perhaps the greatest gift I received from my good friend Ron was the knowledge that this quest for knowledge is singular and requires no rabbi or authority beyond my own inner guide. I would not have discovered this without his support and our extended conversation that lasted for decades and was always anchored in partnership. When we studied or prayed, we did so as equals. Even though his knowledge was far beyond mine and I refer to him as my mentor, when we sat together, we held the space as if we were alone in the world—just two seekers trying to find some trail through the unknown land, each trusting and respecting the other's ideas for the best route through the thicket.

I didn't come to Taos to be Jewish, but here I am in the midst of a thriving community of diverse Jews spanning the spectrum of Orthodox *Chabadniks* to people similar to who I was two decades ago, unaware of their roots or connections. Here in this little valley, there is a raw and robust amalgamation of people searching for authenticity that combines the spectacular natural world of the Taos Valley with ancient tales of the Sinai wilderness. Somewhere in this mix is the juxtaposition of the Taos Pueblo and the way they have preserved their rituals and spiritual values. In some way, knowing that their ceremonies are always taking place validates our ancient tribal wisdom. I can't say exactly how that happens, but I know it to be true. For seven years I worked at the Taos Pueblo as a counselor, and on many occasions I shared my experiences as a Jew with clients as a way to open a dialog about the relationship between faith, values, and service. I discovered that my identity as a Jew was not only accepted, it provided a space where we shared a common mystical lexicon.

It is Friday night, the Sabbath, and we will probably light candles and say a blessing over some wine. Then again, we might not. Instead, I might take a short walk and linger with Cindy as we watch the sunset and appreciate the glory and grandeur of this place and this life we have found in Taos. Regardless, I will be observing with gratitude the sacredness of this site, this Taos, this world—for I will always remember that the only difference between the holy and the profane is the intention that we bring to the moment. As it is said in Genesis 28:16, "Truly, the Eternal is in the place, and I did not know it." Our Jewish community continues to grow and we remain happy and committed.

Part 2

The Taos Rabbis

Rabbi Chavah Carp

"I have gained understanding from all my teachers."
—PSALM 119:99

Rabbi Chavah Carp, born and raised in New York, came to Taos in 1980. She didn't come here to be Jewish. She came to New Mexico because her brother, Joel, was living here at the time. Back then she was Carol Carp and had been living in Chicago. After being in Taos for a year she began looking for the Jewish community and joked that the only Jews she found were in the frozen juice department, right next to the oranges. But she soon discovered that there was a little more going on than she thought.

A group of people were getting together at the House of Taos, a local pizza place. It was led by Ron Kalom. There was another group of six families that included Alyce Frank and Laurel Taub. Everyone got together for Shabbat once in a while. This small group decided they needed something more structured. Laurel Taub knew Rabbi Ted Falcon and contacted him to get some ideas. It was decided that Rabbi Falcon would come to Taos and lead a retreat. The group went through the local phone book and called all the people who had Jewish-sounding last names. To everyone's amazement, more than 100 people attended. It was held at the Young Hunter estate on Piedmont Road, the original home of John Young Hunter, one of the early Taos artists. It was a tremendous success, a day of prayer, study, teaching, and celebration. Rabbi Ted, as he is now known, is a leader in interfaith worship with a special focus on the commonality of spiritual practice, as well as a particular interest in counseling, meditation, and mystical teachings.

The retreat uncovered a thirst for more connection with Judaism. But how? Everyone looked at each other and asked, *What do we do now?* As a group they decided to meet at the Alcalde Building at the Harwood Foundation, which was the Taos Public Library at the time, and figure out the next step. Shortly thereafter the group met again. What happened was something akin to what Chavah called a "military lineup." In response to *What should we do?* everyone stepped back, and she was left standing in front of the line. The truth was, she was the most knowledgeable at the time.

Raised in a Conservative Jewish home; Chavah's mother, Myra, was the principal at the Stephen Wise Free Synagogue in the Upper West Side of New York City. Chavah received her education at the Hebrew

Union College–Jewish Institute of Religion, where she was trained to become a Hebrew and Jewish studies teacher. Given her background, what made the most sense was to start a school. It was 1982.

The first classes met at Mount Wheeler School, which is now the site of The Love Apple restaurant. They later moved to a little house in Talpa, where Chavah was living. It always amazed her that people trusted her enough to leave their children in her tiny adobe home that was without running water or inside plumbing and was lit by a single light bulb in the kitchen. Fortunately, Taos kids at that time were familiar with the use of an outhouse.

When Chavah moved to a more modern home, in Ranchos de Taos, with running water and indoor plumbing, the school moved there as well. The group started holding High Holiday and *Tu BiShvat* services and *seders,* as well as women's Sabbath retreats. By 1989 it became clear that there needed to be some type of formal organization, so Chavah, with the help of Jeff Klein and others, drew up papers to form a nonprofit organization called B'nai Shalom.

At the time, Jeff Klein was married to Consuelo Luz, an aspiring Latin singer with roots in Sephardic Judaism. Chavah introduced Consuelo to the world of ancient Ladino prayers and music and asked her to sing them at some of the services. Later, this experience would lead Consuelo to produce her Sephardic CD, *Dezeo*. Consuelo didn't move to Taos to become Jewish either, yet she is now renowned for her musical accomplishments in Ladino music.

B'nai Shalom held many of its services at St. James Episcopal Church, endearingly known by Mary Nettleton—the wife of the priest—as the *St. James Episcopal Shul*. Mary loved that B'nai Shalom met there and that it became part of an interfaith program in the community. The two congregations greatly appreciated celebrating together.

One festival led to another, and suddenly, there was a regular schedule: High Holidays, Sukkot, Hanukkah, and Passover. Within a span of six or seven years, B'nai Shalom became a community of sixty-five families. From the very beginning B'nai Shalom identified itself as a *havurah*—a Jewish fellowship that meets regularly for discussion and prayer. The Taos Minyan was meeting during this same period, and now there were Jews praying and celebrating all over Taos.

Taos has always been an oasis between the vast altiplano of Northern New Mexico and the majestic peaks of the Sangre de Cristo Mountains, so people living here had to figure things out for themselves. During her early years leading B'nai Shalom, Chavah created rituals for special occasions that until then had not existed. When a local couple wanted to adopt a child and have some type of ceremony with the birth mother, she designed a life-cycle event called the "Exchange of Heartbeats." That kind of spiritually innovative event was something that naturally evolved out of the Taos landscape. One of the more memorable events during this time was the bat mitzvah of Minka Keltz, daughter of Iris and Mark Keltz, held at the Andrew Dasburg Home in Ranchos de Taos. This was a celebration and a weaving together of cultures and Taos history. It was a unique experience to read from the Torah while standing under the power of Taos Mountain.

After being the spiritual leader of B'nai Shalom for several years, Chavah decided it was time for her to become a rabbi. It was 1985. She had heard of Rabbi Zalman Schachter-Shalomi of the Jewish Renewal movement. There was a program available through him. Chavah signed up and began the process of becoming ordained. For several years she traveled back and forth to Philadelphia to study with Rabbi Zalman and others. She also met with teachers and rabbis in Colorado and New Mexico, including Rabbi Tirzah Firestone, Rabbi Gershon Winkler, and Rabbi Shlomo Carlebach. It was a long journey, and while it was happening, she continued to lead B'nai Shalom. In 1993, Chavah Carp became Rabbi Chavah Carp. She received her *semikhah* (ordination—literally, the laying on of hands) from Rabbi Gershom Winkler, who was living in Colorado at the time.

As a newly ordained rabbi, Chavah followed the path of her spiritual guide, Rabbi Zalman Schachter-Shalomi. Rabbi Zalman founded Jewish Renewal to bring a meaningful experience to the celebration of the Jewish life cycle. In an interview in *HaKol*, the Taos Jewish Center's quarterly publication, Rabbi Carp described Jewish Renewal this way:

> There is a term *Chassidut,* which is often used to mean the spiritual or mystical depth to an experience. Reb Zalman Schachter-Shalomi came from an Eastern European background, very Orthodox and highly educated. A piece of his vision for the Renewal movement was to take the traditions of our people and make them accessible to everyone. Often this was done through the use of chanting, movement, and in-depth study. Whether a person is Orthodox, Conservative, Reform, or whatever, Renewal is a possible path to follow. *Na'aseh v'nishma: We will do, and then we will hear the details,* Exodus 24:7. In other words, we are OK doing the rules, but let's find out why, so we can really celebrate with a greater purpose and *kavanah* (heartfelt intention).

Arthur Waskow, a contemporary writer and rabbi, inspired and influenced Rabbi Carp on her rabbinic journey. Waskow was able to transform Jewish traditions and make them more meaningful to a younger generation looking for pathways that encouraged and validated change and openness. His teaching was powerful, and studying with him often, even for short periods of time, would go on for years for Rabbi Carp. Another person she credits with stimulating her Jewish studies was Rabbi Don Singer. Rabbi Singer was ordained at the Hebrew Union College and practiced originally as a traditional Reform Rabbi. Later, he became interested in Zen Buddhism and actually became a teacher of dharma as well as Torah. For Rabbi Carp, he offered a positive way of keeping Jewish teachings very grounded. In 1981, he founded Shir Hadash—a contemplative community of friends open to the dialogue of life.

In 1997, Rabbi Carp decided it was time to step back from her work in Taos, so she moved to Albuquerque, where she started working for Jewish Family Services. From there, she returned to one of her passions: teaching children. She was hired at the Solomon Schechter Day School, located on the campus of the Albuquerque Jewish Community Center. Over the next ten to fifteen years, she also led workshops and helped prepare youth to become bar and bat mitzvah.

Most recently, Rabbi Carp has been active in providing spiritual guidance and leadership in Taos and Northern New Mexico. Currently, she leads monthly Shabbat services for B'nai Shalom Havurah, as well as regular Torah studies. She didn't come to Taos to be Jewish, but she certainly has opened many pathways for children and adults to become deeply involved in the essence of Judaism.

Rabbi Judith HaLevy

"And I will fulfill for you my favorable promise, to return you to this place."
—JEREMIAH 29:10

Rabbi Judith HaLevy came to Taos in 1976, but she didn't arrive as Rabbi Judith, nor did she come to Taos to be Jewish. She was driving with a friend who needed a ride to the Lama Foundation. She had been living in Tepoztlán, a small municipality south of Mexico City that is reputed to be the birthplace of Quetzalcoatl, the Aztec feathered serpent god. At the time, she was married to Elly Kraiem, an Israeli who was directing the Centro Deportivo Israelita, which is the largest Jewish community center in Mexico. She had spent six years in Mexico and had two children eighteen months apart.

Things were good and things were not good. The marriage had ended, and it was time to leave Mexico and move to Taos—not be Jewish, but to find a place for her two young children to live and get an education. When she arrived at the Lama Foundation, she met Asha Durkee, one of its founders. Judith fell in love with Lama.

As it is often said, Taos Mountain either accepts you and your Taos path is smooth, or it spits you out and sends you packing.

While Lama was a compelling spiritual environment, it was no place to raise two young children. Asha said, "You can't live here with your two little ones. I can get you a job at Da Nahazli (Navajo for eternal spring) School, where your kids can go for free." Da Nahazli would later become the Taos Valley School, where I was headmaster during the early '80s. Da Nahazli was a reincarnation of A.S. Neill Summerhill School but with a Taos hippie flavor, where no kids had matching socks. Judith's plan was to use Taos as a transitional space for, at most, a year, and then either move back to the East Coast or Israel. The transition took eighteen years.

After a year at Da Nahazli, getting a paltry $400 per month, Judith was hired at Taos High School. Being bilingual gave her an immediate inside track to pick out whatever courses she wanted to teach. She spent eight years at THS, teaching both bilingual education and her real love, drama. Together with Nancy Jenkins, another legendary Taos educator, they produced numerous high-quality theater productions on the Taos stage. Little did she know that all her theater experience would later come to serve her as a rabbi.

While Judith did not come to Taos be Jewish, she did have a son and a daughter who would need to become bar and bat mitzvah. Daniela was the eldest. It happened that when Daniela turned twelve, Judith was attending a workshop at Lama led by none other than Rabbi Shlomo Carlebach, known as "the singing rabbi." Carlebach, trained as a traditional Hasidic rabbi, had become famous for his folk renderings of traditional Hebrew songs. He also pioneered the *Baal Teshuva* movement that encouraged disenchanted Jews to return to the fold through song and meaningful ritual. It was in that spirit that Reb Shlomo asked Judith where in the wilds of New Mexico was she going to get a bat mitzvah for her daughter who had become of age. Judith's son Eliam was already studying with Ron, but Dani was not. "Bring her up," he offered, "and we will do her bat mitzvah on Shabbat."

As Judith tells it, "All she could do at the time was recite a few prayers, but the fifty or so participants covered her with blessings for strength as a young Jewish woman in a changing world, and I believe it led to her career in working for women's rights." Currently, Daniela leads the program of Gender and Law at American University Law School.

Meanwhile, Eliam continued his study with Ron Kalom. Judith had met Ron shortly after she arrived in Taos when she cast him as Tevye in the local production of *Fiddler on the Roof*. She and Ron bonded immediately, and the friendship lasted until Ron died in 2019. Ron prepared Eliam for his bar mitzvah, and he would later serve as one of Judith's many mentors on her path to becoming a rabbi.

As the years went on, Judith became more involved in the Taos Jewish community, both with B'nai Shalom and creating events on her own. Often someone was needed to lead a service or officiate at a Jewish event, and Judith stepped forward. Her desire for more Jewish knowledge grew and deepened. For many years she studied every Shabbat afternoon with Sue Ann Lasker. In addition to Torah, they studied Kabbalah, and Sue Ann, an artist, created a series of paintings of the Jewish alphabet. Judith's study led her to connect with teachers and rabbis. One of those was Rabbi Zalman Schachter-Shalomi, who had been at the Lama Foundation and whom Judith had met at other conferences.

Later, she was introduced to another rabbi, Jonathan Omer-Man, who had been described by a friend as "the spiritual rabbi" and someone she had to meet. In 1984, after having met Rabbi Omer-Man in Santa Fe, she called him and asked if she could study with him privately. At the time, she didn't realize his prominence in the world of Judaism. He agreed, and so began an eight-year journey that changed her life. The reality was that she actually became his apprentice, studying with him once a week by phone. Together, they deeply explored Jewish texts. He became her guide for the Jewish services she was doing in Taos.

Having lived in Israel between 1968 and 1971, Judith had a comfortable working knowledge of Hebrew, which served as a foundation for further study with Rabbi Omer-Man. Whenever she had a free weekend, she traveled to Los Angeles to study with him and participate in his work there. To this day, her work with him provides the underpinnings of all she does as a rabbi. Through this privileged relationship, Judith was able to glean great spiritual insights that would otherwise not have been available. In 1991, Rabbi Omer-Man founded Metivta, a center for contemplative Judaism, an academy dedicated to the renewal of traditional Jewish meditation and to the deepening of personal religious quest. On her visits to Los Angeles, Judith spent a great deal of time leading and participating in the activities at the center.

What became unique about her odyssey into the world of becoming a rabbi was her Taos experience. Although she didn't realize it when she first came to Northern New Mexico, this place under Taos Mountain engendered a particular sensibility. In her experience, Taos is a sacred place. Being here gave her a rare perspective that she has been able to incorporate into her work. She resonated with the vistas, the extraordinary sunsets, the Rio Grande Gorge, the Lama Foundation, the art and creative spirit that seemed to imbue all those who live here and, most importantly, the continual flow of seekers who came to Taos—not particularly to be Jewish, but to certainly discover something new about themselves. This pulse of energy was the force that Judith recognized as the magic of Taos, and it is what helped contribute to her brilliance as a rabbi.

By 1990, Judith knew that she would be ordained. Her work with Rabbi Omer-Man continued, but her opportunities in Taos for rabbinic work were limited. Almost simultaneously, she was offered a job with the Santa Fe Chamber Music Festival as well as a rabbinic internship at Temple Beth Shalom in Santa Fe. As fate would have it, the rabbi at the temple lost his job, and there was Judith. She took over as the interim rabbi while the congregation did their search. Meanwhile, she suddenly became the leader of largest temple in Santa Fe. It was a huge responsibility, and she managed to take charge and hold the congregation together while the search moved forward. It took almost a year.

She was ordained in 1992 in Santa Fe at Temple Beth Shalom. Rabbi Omer-Man did the service, and afterward he said to her, "You are now a 51 percent rabbi. And as Rabbi Hillel said, 'Now go and study.'" It was Rabbi Omer-Man's first *semikhah*, and it is chronicled on page 210 in Rodger Kamenetz's book *The Jew in the Lotus*. After the ordination, she moved to Los Angeles to help Rabbi Jonathon with Metivta, a center for contemplative Judaism, which had just received some additional funding.

Leaving Taos was one thing, leaving New Mexico proved to be more of a challenge. It is hard to imagine two more different places than Taos and Los Angeles. In thinking back about that time in her life, Rabbi Judith refers to it as a time of exile, but that story of exile quickly became a story of transformation. She worked closely with Rabbi Jonathan and together they developed programs and offered study groups and retreats with a focus on Jewish meditation and spirituality. The experience enriched her skills and helped develop her confidence as a spiritual leader.

From that formative experience, two communities came into being. One was Metivta, and the other was Sarah's Tent, which she started very soon after arriving in Los Angeles. It was a women's program, and the timing and place were perfect. Her own experience as a creative Jewish woman gave her the wisdom to put together a transcendent experience that was like a theater but with Rabbi Nachman stories. Looking back on those years with Sarah's Tent, Rabbi HaLevy attributes its success to her time in Taos: "the Taos magic."

Sarah's Tent was held mostly in Los Angeles, but there were retreats in Taos as well.

It was incredibly difficult to leave Taos; she has said that it was as if a part of her had been left behind. The initial feeling of exile reminded her of similar feelings she had experienced when she left Israel. This was a period akin to the biblical wanderings in the book of Exodus. Metivta and Sarah's Tent were the grounding forces that kept her going in Los Angeles.

For a few years Sarah's Tent provided a sufficient community; it was an exhilarating experience, combining feminism, art, theater, and Torah all under one pavilion. As enchanting as it was, it didn't pay the bills. So she began looking for other gigs. The best-paying job for an unaffiliated rabbi is leading High Holiday services, so that's where she looked. The Malibu Jewish Center, a Reconstructionist congregation, had been without a rabbi for eighteen months and needed one for the holidays. Rabbi Judith submitted her résumé, and they called her in for an "audition service." Right away, they offered her a full-time position and wanted her to start immediately. But she had already committed to a Sarah's Tent retreat in Taos and she told the board they would have to wait until the retreat was over, in two weeks. The retreat ended and the board got back in touch and told her that they couldn't wait any longer. She had twenty-four hours or they were going to offer the job to a rabbi from Hong Kong, Howard Kosovske. Sylvia Borstein—a well-known writer and meditation teacher, as well as a close friend of Rabbi Judith—had been with her at the retreat. Her advice was, "Well, whaddya got to lose? Get in the car. Go. Do it. *Lech Lecha.* If you hate it, you will quit." Sage spiritual advice.

Rabbi Judith got in the car and, once again, left Taos, only this time it was for a very specific purpose. That was 1997. The part-time gig that she was after lasted two decades. During that time, she became an esteemed and well-respected Jewish leader in the world of Southern California rabbis. She served as a member of the executive committee of the Board of Rabbis of Southern California and was the president of the board from 2011 to 2013. Her dedication to study led her to the Shalom Hartman Institute in Jerusalem in 2007, where she is currently one of the esteemed senior members. The Shalom Hartman Institute is a leading center of Jewish thought and education, serving Israel and North America. With a focus on Judaism and modernity, as well as democratic rights for all people in Israel, the Hartman Institute each year brings together the finest Jewish scholars, theologians, and writers to focus on contemporary issues facing the Jewish people.

Rabbi Judith retired from the Malibu Jewish Center in 2017, which honored her with the title of Rabbi

Emerita of that organization. As Alexander Graham Bell once said, "When one door closes, another opens." Or, as Bob Marley sang it, "When one door is closed, don't you know another is open?"

At almost that exact time, Rabbi Paul Citrin completed his service at the Taos Jewish Center, and they were looking for a rabbi. Coming back to Taos had always been the ultimate dream for Judith. The Hebrew word *bashert* means both destiny and soul mate. To say that it was *bashert* that the Taos Jewish Center was searching for a rabbi at the same moment that Judith was retiring from MJC meets both definitions. Taos had always been her geographic soul mate. At the time, I was part of the search committee, and when I found out that Judith was possibly available, especially as a part-time rabbi, I told the committee I thought our search was over. There were details to work out, but after Rabbi Judith came and did one Shabbat service, the TJC community knew that, indeed, it was *bashert* and we had a match.

As of this writing, Rabbi Judith has been the spiritual leader of the Taos Jewish Center since 2018. Her accomplishments in building community endure. The Sarah's Tent project continues to thrive and the participants stay in touch, even though they are spread across the country. There is research being done that might lead to a book and, recently, Judith conducted a series of interviews that may lead to a feature-length documentary film.

The Kotzker de Taos
Ron Kalom

"People tend to look upwards, contemplating the mysteries of the heavens. They would do well to look inward and examine what's happening within themselves."

"He who doesn't see G-d everywhere isn't capable of seeing Him anywhere."

"There is nothing so whole as a broken heart."
—Rabbi Menachem Mendel of Kotzk

In the northeast corner of the Eretz Shalom Cemetery in Taos, there is a headstone engraved with the words "Kotzker de Taos." It isn't the gravesite of Rabbi Menachem Mendel. It is the resting place of Ron Kalom. Ron had always been an admirer of the famous Rabbi of Kotzk, but at some point in his life, I'm not sure when, he adopted the title of "The Kotzker de Taos." For a brief period, he wrote a series of poignant articles for *HaKol,* the TJC periodical that, at the time, was under the editorial direction of Karl Halpert. Ron used a nom de plume, *The Kotzker.*

Rabbi Menachem Mendel had lived in Poland from 1787 to 1859. He was a brilliant, uncompromising, and demanding Chasidic teacher. His desire to live a life of deep inner truth, along with his quest for perfection, limited his following. Toward the end of his life, Rabbi Mendel spent a great deal of his time in solitude, peering into the depths of what it meant to be a righteous human being. While Rabbi Mendel wrote voluminously, he ordered most everything he wrote to be burned, but what has survived is a compilation of his words in the form of maxims that are as profound as anything ever written.

Ron Kalom arrived in Taos on October 5, 1968, not in search of how to become the Taos Kotzker, but simply looking for a place to escape the craziness of the what had happened at the Democratic Convention in Chicago during the summer of that year. Together with the love of his life, Carolyn, and their young daughter, Noelle, they loaded as much as they could into their VW Bug and plowed through the Midwest until they reached Boulder, Colorado. The beautiful landscape of the Rockies held them for only a long weekend. Ron had a passionate interest in D.H. Lawrence and a strong desire to explore the place where Lawrence had once lived: Taos, New Mexico. He knew there was some kind of Lawrence memorial site north of Taos, and he wanted to visit it. Whether it was love at first sight or whether it took a while for the Taos magic to take hold isn't clear; what is certain is that Taos became his home for next fifty-one years.

With a family to feed, the first problem he encountered was how to make a living. One night, after a disappointing dinner at a place called Big Brad's, Ron ran outside and shouted at the moon, "Even I can do better than that!" Shortly after, he and Carolyn, having no real experience in the restaurant business, opened The House of Taos, a pizzeria. On May 1, 1969, they celebrated Ron's thirty-fifth birthday with free pizza for friends and neighbors and officially opened the business the next day. It was located in Guadalupe Plaza, the row of buildings that face the parking lot west of the Taos Plaza. Not only did the eatery become successful, it also became a social hub for the artists, writers, and actors who were looking for a place to gather. Ron had been a social worker in Chicago and had a natural inclination to help others, so The House of Taos also became an unofficial counseling center.

Ron definitely did not come to Taos to be Jewish, but Judaism dwelt within him like a sacred spring. He grew up in Evanston, Illinois, just north of Chicago, attending the progressive Francis Parker School on the north side. At the same time, he began his Jewish education under the guidance of Rabbi David Polish, founder of the first Reform congregation in Evanston—Beth Emet, The Free Synagogue. The name Free Synagogue refers to the commitment to freedom of speech from the pulpit, a right that Rabbi Polish was denied on his former dais. Rabbi Polish advocated for freedom, whether it was for Israel or the rights of Black Americans. In 1958, long before it was fashionable for Jews to support Black American rights, Rabbi Polish invited the Reverend Doctor Martin Luther King Jr. to speak and preach at the temple. It was in this liberal, activist environment that Ron gained his knowledge of Jewish learning. After his bar mitzvah, he led youth groups and became a mentor for many children in the community.

After graduating from Francis Parker School, Ron joined the army. The Korean war was still simmering, and rather than get drafted, he signed up and served in Europe. The ashes of the Holocaust were still warm, and his proximity to the camps left a lifelong memory that, at times, became a kind of obsession. He never forgot. Following three years of service, he returned home and attended school under the G.I. Bill at Roosevelt University, studying English literature, but that did not lead to anything satisfying.

Instead, he decided it was time to pursue his interest in Judaism and discover whether he had what it took to become a rabbi. The Hebrew Union College in Cincinnati accepted his application, and off he went.

After a year of study, he came to the realization that a career in the rabbinate was not his heart's desire. It was now his time of "wandering." He had met and married an Israeli woman, Tamara, and they decided to move to Israel. Living and working in the Jewish homeland became his true immersion into the life and culture of his heritage, and yet his calling as a teacher was still far off in a distant part of the world.

The marriage ended, and he returned to Chicago, where he found a job as a social worker in an area that had a lot of gang activity. At the same time, he got involved in theater and met Carolyn, who would become his life partner. Always a hard and dedicated worker, he found ways to communicate with and help his clients. The work satisfied him, but the social and political environment in Chicago at that time ate away at his soul, so he and Carolyn decided to move west.

When I asked Ron in our 2011 interview for *HaKol* what the Jewish landscape was like when he arrived in 1968, he said, "Well, you might say it was a barren desert. There was a Jewish doctor named Al Rosen, a surgeon who had done a couple of *brit milahs* (ritual circumcisions). Dr. Rosen, an avid skier was a close friend of Ernie Blake, founder of the Taos Ski Valley. Blake named the infamous steep run at the ski area Al's Run, after Dr. Rosen. There was a fellow named Irving Greene and his wife Hadassah, but these were business people and, as far as I know, they didn't have anything Jewish organized in Taos."

The first services Ron led were in the dining room of The House of Taos in the late '60s. A ragtag group gathered, and they used the old, conservative Birnbaum Siddur, a prayer book first published in 1949. From the beginning, Ron's way of leading (or not leading) a group in prayer was for everyone to stand together and *daven* (pray) in unison. They met every Saturday as long as they had at least three or four people present. Sometimes, it was just Ron and one or two others. It was a very informal arrangement. Hank Saxe was one of the regulars, along with Harvey Kalmeyer, who later moved to Denver. That was how it started.

When Passover came, the group wondered what to do about a *seder*. The first one was held in a little coffeehouse on Guadalupe Plaza run by the Bergerson brothers, Marc and Rick. Marc was a well-known Taos abstract artist, and Rick was a plumbing contractor. Later, the *seders* moved to The House of Taos. But what to do about the *Haggadah?* In the beginning, they searched for a *Haggadah* that would have relevance to their lives in Taos, but nothing seemed to fit. Ron, along with a few other members of the group—including Dan Ross, a journalist for the *Taos News*, and Rick Bergerson—cobbled together a little book and called it "The West Side Haggadah." Dan Ross went on to write

Acts of Faith, published by St. Martin's Press, about journeys into the fringes of Jewish identity. Inside Ron's copy of the book, Dan inscribed the following, "This book was born in your house."

Ron called it the "West Side Haggadah" as a joke. It identified the part of Taos where he lived, west of the plaza, and the old Jewish part of Chicago, west of Roosevelt Road. This was the location of the famous Maxwell Street Market. The inaugural *seder* was held on April 6, 1974. Since that time there have been numerous incarnations of Ron's original *Haggadah*, including the one used at the Taos Jewish Center and, of course, the one Cindy and I use each year.

From the age of fifteen, Ron led Jewish services in one form or another. It was his natural calling, and he continued guiding the Jewish spirit until his breath and body could no longer do it. Along the way, he trained youth and prepared them to become a bar or bat mitzvah. His first student was Eliam Kraiem, the son of Rabbi Judith HaLevy. Shortly thereafter he prepared Lucas Schreiber, the son of Dr. Larry Schreiber, for his bar mitzvah. Ron distilled the natural flow of Jewish study into a few basic concepts that allowed his students to comprehend the essential liturgy of a prayer service.

Ron believed that the centerpiece of a prayer service consisted of two observances, the *Shema* and the

Shemoneh Esrei, also known as the *Amidah,* the standing prayer. If you learn and understand those two, the rest is just embellishment, except for the *Kaddish.* Ron's students learned to put the Hebrew alphabet into their mouths and souls so the letters became pathways to meaning, and from there, the experience became embedded in their memory; hopefully, the recollection of the sight and sound of those prayers would remain forever. All his students affirm the impact he had upon their comprehension of Jewish prayer in the context of both daily worship and annual celebrations. By example, he stressed a particular ethos: preparation, intention, truthfulness, memory, and humility. Within prayer services, he shared his wisdom without restraint or judgment and always had an uncanny ability to include and teach to the one who knew the least, while at the same time honoring and respecting those who knew more.

And then there was the calendar—a handwritten annual remembrance of the days in a large 12×17-inch format that cataloged memorials, birthdays, anniversaries, and historical events. Ron's friend, the late architect Bill Mingenbach, called this creation the *Kalomdar.* The list included immediate and extended family and friends; historical characters, like Emerson and Maimonides; community members of significance; and sacred events, such as bar and bat mitzvahs. The calendar served as a script for his day and included phones calls, personal visits, handwritten cards, or, if you were lucky, a letter. A prolific letter writer, Ron honed his craft into a form that was sophisticated, witty, heartfelt, and filled with treasures. He was generous in sending out his missives. I was astonished to discover that for years he had been writing letters to my parents, and upon their passing, I found these treasures carefully put away in a box labeled "Save for Bruce." At his memorial, many spoke of the letters they had saved over the years.

Ron kept track of everything. The spiritual significance of this exercise emphasized his regard for the role of memory in every facet of life and history. At his memorial, his close friend, the writer John Nichols, quoted a line from Phillip Roth's book *Patrimony:* "You must not forget anything." For Ron the rabbi, the Jew, the writer, and the friend, memory held meaning and served as a beacon for truth, intimacy, and understanding. The depth of his remembrance—whether it was the date of the opening of the new Taos Public Library, the anniversary of his friends David and Mary Raskin (whom he and his wife, Carolyn, brunched with every Sunday), or the liberation of the death camps—informed and enriched his daily life. In particular, the memory of the Holocaust held a special place in Ron's world. When November 9 rolled around on the

Kalomdar, I would often get a phone call from Ron, notifying me that it was the anniversary of Kristallnacht. He would go on about how, even to this day, the sound of glass breaking disturbed him because of the association with windows of Jewish homes and businesses being shattered.

April 19 on the Kalomdar marked the beginning of the Warsaw Ghetto Uprising. Ron gathered that reminiscence and carried it around for the day, telling anyone who would take the time to listen that we must not forget those brave Jews and what their sacrifice meant. You might run into him in the fruit and vegetable section at Cid's Food Market on January 27, and he'd inform you that this was the day that Auschwitz was liberated. In that moment, between the celery and the grapefruit, you would need to pause with Ron and savor that recollection. Ron didn't come to Taos to take on the role of a rabbi or even to be a Jew, but whether it was in the post office or the supermarket or around the study table, he exuded a prophetic honesty that awakened you out of your mundane wonderings. The Kalomdar was one of the things that helped him keep his focus.

Ron ordered the calendars in bulk and started writing down each event months before the New Year. It took a long time because there were so many people and memories to catalog. That he took the time to recreate the Kalomdar every year reflects his intention and purpose. He was the ultimate Taos scribe, and he did it because his personal values motivated him to maintain an impeccable integrity when it came to honoring relationships, whether those be with individuals or historic moments. Elie Wiesel, mentor of memory and someone Ron Kalom often quoted, said, "To be Jewish is to remember—to claim our right to memory as well as our duty to keep it alive."

Two weeks after the bar mitzvah of Teo Grossman on June 25, 1993, a small group gathered at Ted Dimond's house for the first of what would be a twenty-year run of the Taos Minyan. The first group was quite small, but it grew and morphed over the years. Although Ron refused to formally acknowledge his role as the rabbi of the group, there was never any doubt that he not only carried the tune during the prayers, but he carried the authority of knowledge as well as the consistency; in all the years we met, he never missed a service. Looking back, he instinctively knew what to do from the start, yet he let everyone discover their own path. Never standing in the front of the group, he positioned himself somewhere within so the sound and rhythm of his chanting emanated as if coming from the heart of the gathering rather than the head. He told everyone from the start that we need not try to recreate the wheel, the dynamics of what a minyan did were rudimentary. It mattered more that whatever we did, we did with heartfelt intention.

The Hebrew prayers themselves were ancient and had survived centuries of attack and banishment. We just needed to infuse them with our own breath, and the rest would happen naturally. On that first morning, we opened the traditional Reform Siddur, called the "Gates of Prayer," and read through the pages until we arrived at the Torah service. As always, Ron knew what to do. In the beginning, we did not have a Torah, and no one had any intention or wish to acquire one. But we all had and used English translations of the Torah. At Ron's suggestion, we took turns reading through the passages of the weekly portion. From the very beginning, Ron came prepared with his own personal commentary that was either handwritten or typed on one of his manual typewriters. The pages were dense, single-spaced if typed; if handwritten, the writing was clear but in relatively small script. On average, what he wrote amounted to three to five pages. Well organized and researched, complete with quotes and references, his pieces were part sermon, part op-ed, part scholarly treatise, and part poetry.

Yet, even with his superior skill and intellect, Ron's humility and generosity of spirit motivated all who attended to offer their own perspectives, ideas, and disagreements. Questions were always encouraged and respected. Ron held the belief that there were no stupid questions. He was Socratic at his core; inquiry formed the basis of his theology. His close friend George Malko eulogized him in this way:

> I did, on one of our visits, ask him if all of those years had answered any of his questions. Ron said that wasn't what one was supposed to get from studies and readings. What was it, then? More questions, he said. I asked if that was the basis—cultural, historic, ethnic, what have you—of the classic Jewish joke: Why does a Jew always answer a question with a question? His reply: Why not?

"The task of the Torah teacher is to render his services unnecessary; his task is not to keep students dependent." That quote from Rabbi Samson Raphael Hirsch, a nineteenth-century scholar, sums up how Ron viewed his role as a teacher. Often in our conversations, Ron mused that he was born in the wrong century. His epoch of choice was to be beside Emerson and Hirsch during a time when the pace of life was slower, letters were all handwritten, and time for conversation had fewer constraints. In preparing his notes for the minyan he applied his philosophy about writing. "A personal address deserves a relaxed and slow shepherding of one's potential during that mysterious encounter when pen meets paper." He brought that nineteenth-century sensibility into the minyan, where, for a few hours each week, there was a feeling of being cloistered in a timeless chamber in which minds and souls engaged in the ancient art of spiritual inquiry.

The one rabbi that influenced Ron more than any other was Abraham Joshua Heschel, who marched beside Martin Luther King Jr. in Selma, Alabama, in March 1965. It was during this march that Heschel made his famous remark that he felt like his legs were praying.

Heschel and King had a deep connection, and King considered him his rabbi and a man with prophetic insights. The combination of social and political action, as well as Heschel's keen theological and philosophical prowess, made him the perfect model for Ron. Born in Warsaw in 1907, Heschel is considered one of the great philosophers and theologians of the twentieth century. In his later years. Ron quoted Heschel, saying, "Never in my life did I ask God for success or wisdom or power or fame. I asked for wonder, and He gave it to me." Warsaw is a long way from Taos, and even though Ron didn't come to Taos to be Jewish, he brought Heschel with him and imparted the great man's wisdom to all who stood beside him.

Along with Heschel and Rabbi Mendel, there was one other profound influence on Ron, and that was

Shlomo Carlebach, the renowned troubadour of Jewish "soul music." Carlebach visited Taos on several occasions, but Ron met him while attending Hebrew Union College in Cincinnati, and they had a "pretty tight relationship." Carlebach played in coffeehouses in New York City, where he encountered and was encouraged by the likes of Pete Seeger and Bob Dylan. An Orthodox Jew by training, Carlebach used his guitar and his creativity to transform traditional liturgy into a new contemporary sound that resonated with the '60s generation and began an entirely new way of approaching prayer and celebration. Ron incorporated this new style into his own chants, which became part of his services and *liberated* his voice so all could enjoy and appreciate an original rendering of traditional liturgy.

Ron said, "Prayer is yearning to escape from the limitations of our own weakness and an invocation for all good to enter and abide within us." What makes a great teacher is authenticity, connection, knowledge, and imagination. Ron had all those qualities, along with humility. The mantle he wore was neither a suit nor a robe. His lack of pretense preceded him in everything he did. He could have been a "real" rabbi—of that there is no doubt, but the path he chose was the inscrutable and the paradoxical. "We don't need a rabbi," he often said. "It's Taos. We can do this ourselves; we are doing it ourselves." He respected most rabbis for their work and dedication and maintained good relationships with all who passed through or lived in the valley. His work remained personal in his daily study and worship, yet when called upon for a service, a funeral, a wedding, or a bat/bar mitzvah, he responded with the biblical *Hineni* (Here I am). Always ready to serve, always ready to give: it was the way he lived. As Jewish life in Taos got more involved, it felt like there was so much to do and, at the same time, nothing ever seemed finished. Ron wrote this:

> None of us—not even you
> Were engaged to complete the task.
> Not one of us will be penalized
> For being unable to finish.
> We gave—hopefully—our best efforts
> To serve the task of ongoing creation.
> We did not approach TORAH
> As an optional duty.
> The few—it is always the few—
> Shouldered the burden.
> Full effort we gave
> Not seeking success
> We persevered with full hearts
> Doing our parts.
> The work was great, and faithfully
> We did strive to perform our allotted tasks.
> All the work we could never do

All that we did not do
We leave in the Hands of God.

He signed it *The Kotzker.*

Part 3

The Gatherings

B'nai Shalom Havurah

"Who finds a faithful friend, finds a treasure."
—JEWISH PROVERB

In the beginning there was a barren wilderness, void of anything Jewish. No one specifically came to Taos to be Jewish, yet they were here. People met in restaurants, libraries, and individual homes, and asked one another, *What do we do? There is no school, no one to lead the High Holiday services, and what about Passover?* They met and wondered how anyone could be Jewish in such a place without a synagogue or a Jewish community center or even a Jewish delicatessen.

As Rabbi Chavah Carp tells it, several Jewish families had been meeting informally since the early '80s, and she had been running a Jewish school for children in the community. By 1989, it became clear to Chavah—as well as others, like Jeff Klein—that a more formal group was needed. Jeff and Chavah set up a nonprofit called B'nai Shalom Havurah. They formed a board of directors and began observing the major Jewish holidays, including monthly Sabbath service and

Torah study. Services were held in people's homes, and when there was a need for a larger space, they used the St. James Episcopal Church, where they were always warmly welcomed by Father Ed Nettleton and his wife, Mary. From the very start, Ed and Mary were strong supporters of B'nai Shalom. Even though they have since moved to Colorado, the relationship between B'nai Shalom and the Episcopal church remains strong and fosters an ongoing commitment to interfaith projects in the Taos community.

For almost three decades, Bette Myerson has been a guiding force for B'nai Shalom. She came to Taos for the light and sunshine. Bette had been living in the Bay Area, and the foggy, damp weather had started to take its toll. Her former Spanish teacher and friend, Shirley, lived in Taos and invited her for a visit. It was the end of March 1984, and she was ready for a change. After visiting Flagstaff, Sedona, and Santa Fe, she arrived in Taos. Shirley was thrilled to see Bette, and Taos Mountain graced and welcomed her. Although Bette did not come to Taos to be Jewish, she reached out to the B'nai Shalom community in an effort to connect and meet people. In college, she had been president of the Wellesley Hillel and had been confirmed as a teen in the Reform tradition, so she was familiar with the world of Jewish life. At first she didn't find what she was seeking. After spending some time with Chavah

Carp, they became close friends. Chavah asked her to be on the board. Bette accepted and soon became a respected leader and spokesperson for the group. Her intuitive ability to work with people and her experience working with other nonprofits soon made her an invaluable asset to the organization.

Bette found a position with Mountain Home Health Care for a whopping five dollars per hour, but before long her expertise in finance together with her indefatigable dedication elevated her to the position of finance director, which she retained for almost thirty years. Meanwhile, Bette anchored the B'nai Shalom board and consistently developed programs for those in need. When Bobbi Shapiro, another board member, suggested that the group form a *mitzvah* fund to help those in need in Taos, Bette helped make it a reality. Later, when Kathleen Burg was looking for another sponsor for the *Chesed* project, now known as Artstreams, Bette offered B'nai Shalom as a fiscal agent for the organization. More recently, with Bette's help and energy, B'nai Shalom has supported Taos Immigrant Allies, helping many immigrant families get settled in New Mexico.

B'nai Shalom provides unique opportunities to honor traditional Jewish commemorations. For several decades, Bette, under the auspices of B'nai Shalom, has sponsored a *Succoth* celebration at her home. The entire Taos Jewish community is always welcome. Everyone is invited to bring things to decorate the *sukkah* (shelter). Celebrating this festive holiday in Bette's backyard exemplifies the warm, generous, and communal spirit of B'nai Shalom. Monthly Shabbat services are held every third Friday. The schedule is set this way intentionally so as not to conflict with the Taos Jewish Center Shabbat services that are held on the second and fourth weekends of the month.

During the winter season, B'nai Shalom co-sponsors the Peace Chanukah celebration. Once again, Bette has been the lead person in organizing the event. For many years, she has been deeply involved in interfaith pathways. A lover of music, Bette has been a member of the St. James Episcopal choir for decades. Peace Chanukah offers a unique way of joining people of many faiths to move us closer to *tikkun olam* (the repair of the world). Of Peace Chanukah, Bette was quoted in the *Taos News*:

> You certainly don't have to have any kind of religious background or be associated with any kind of spiritual group to participate in this event. The messages people will be speaking of are of faith and hope and love. The idea of goodness and kindness is not just related to religion. It's something

that many people can believe in. We have lots of people who come who are not associated with religious practice. Everyone is welcome. This is about community. This is about our Taos community and spreading love and kindness and support to each other and everyone in our midst.

Unlike many Jewish organizations, including the Taos Jewish Center, B'nai Shalom does not have membership dues. In part, this is in deference to the fact that TJC needs more regular funding to support and maintain the physical plant that provides for a Jewish space, as well as a home for the library and the three Torah scrolls.

In 1971, Bonnie Korman and her husband, Bob Bishop, moved to Taos—not to be Jewish but to follow the zeitgeist of the late 1960s.

"We weren't exactly hippies, but some of our best friends were," Bonnie related. "Like many folks at that time, we were definitely political activists."

With their four-month-old son Jonah in tow, they followed their friends Joe Caldwell and Judy Lockwood, who also had a young son, Max, to Taos. Joe had family in Northern New Mexico and was actually born in Springer. Bob had been through Taos once, but only for a day.

Bonnie and Bob were enchanted by the mountain, the views, and the people. Before long they became friends with many of the Taos locals, including Jo Carey, Gene Weisfeld, and Taos author John Nichols, who lived in their neighborhood. Bonnie was already familiar with the Southwest, having grown up in Texas, where her family had resided for several generations, descendants of the early immigrants who had been part of the Galveston Plan—an immigration policy during the early twentieth century that diverted Jewish immigrants from East Coast cities, who were already facing housing problems, to the port of Galveston. Many Jews, like Bonnie's family, remained in Texas, while others settled in cities in the South and Midwest.

Bonnie was not particularly looking for a Jewish community, but she had a rich background and education in the tradition. Her grandparents were Orthodox, and Bonnie attended services regularly and was confirmed as a young teen. When she arrived in Taos, the only Jewish activities were what Ron Kalom was doing at the House of Taos.

Chavah Carp arrived in Taos just around the time that Bob and Bonnie's son Jonah and daughter Maria were ready for some kind of Jewish education. Bonnie enrolled her children in Chavah's Sunday school, and they soon became friends. Before long, the school evolved into a larger community that would become B'nai Shalom. Jonah continued to study with Chavah, and, when the time came for his bar mitzvah, Chavah joined with Rabbi Lynn Gottlieb to officiate at the ceremony. By now Chavah was on her path to becoming a rabbi and was studying with Rabbi Zalman Schachter-Shalomi. Bonnie was familiar with all the traditional forms of Judaism; Reform, Conservative, and Orthodox. But B'nai Shalom and Chavah were now exploring another path called Renewal. Bonnie became one of the first board members of B'nai Shalom. She was inspired by Chavah's journey that led to her rabbinic ordination. Bonnie described it as one of the peak experiences of her life. "The reality that a woman, a strong and powerful woman, could become a rabbi really resonated with me."

One of the most astonishing stories in the history of B'nai Shalom was how this fledging *havurah* acquired a Holocaust Torah. After their official formation, B'nai Shalom started having Shabbat and High Holiday services. When the time came to read from the Torah, they used different volumes and translations. At one point they had a discussion about wanting a Torah scroll to make the services more authentic. As a result, Rabbi Carp recalls, Jeff Klein found out about the Memorial Scrolls Trust and started to research the possibility of getting one for B'nai Shalom.

Jeff discovered that the Holocaust scrolls were never sold or donated; instead, they were permanently loaned, as long as the congregation used and cared for them. Still, there were significant costs involved, such as shipping, handling, insurance, and associated administrative fees. Jeff also found out that not many Torahs were still available. So B'nai Shalom needed to act speedily. The group had to come up with $500—a significant amount for B'nai Shalom at that time. Rabbi Carp remembers sending out a fundraising letter, hopeful that the community would respond quickly.

Once again, it was Roger Lerman who led the way and contributed the first check. After that the money started to flow and, within a short time, there was $1,000 in the bank. Arrangements were made for the shipping, papers were signed, and in 1983 the Taos Jewish community received its first Torah scroll. Once the Torah arrived, Roger wasted no time in crafting a perfect cedar ark that protected it and made it easy to transport from home to home. He also fashioned a small battery-operated *ner tamid* (eternal light) to set atop the ark.

A detailed history of these scrolls can be found online. You will discover a fascinating story chronicling the Nazi invasion of Czechoslovakia and how hundreds of Torahs were confiscated, cataloged, and warehoused. After the war, the British discovered the trove of holy scrolls. Initially, the Brits attempted to return the scrolls to their rightful communities, but almost all of those congregations no longer existed. The complete story of how the scrolls came to London can be found in the book *Out of the Midst of Fire*, by Philippa Bernard, available at the TJC Library. The Torah scrolls were eventually brought to the Westminster Synagogue in London, in 1964. The Memorial Scrolls Trust was created to care for, repair, and find homes for these orphaned Torahs.

B'nai Shalom remains a vital and important part of the Taos Jewish community. Over the years, it has contributed material and spiritual support to Jews and non-Jews throughout Northern New Mexico. Under the dynamic leadership of current President Annette Rubin, the rest of the B'nai Shalom board continue to sustain many worthy causes that help promote *tikkun olam* (repairing the world). Lastly, we are so fortunate to have B'nai Shalom as the trusted guardians and fiscal sponsors of the Eretz Shalom Cemetery, which remains the only freestanding Jewish cemetery in New Mexico.

The Taos Minyan

"For I have given you a good teaching;
do not forsake my Torah."
—Proverbs 4:2

The Taos Minyan had a profound effect in shaping my connection to Judaism. It began June 25, 1993, in the home of Ted Dimond, and was the natural culmination of a spontaneous spark of interest in Torah study among several individuals. Two weeks earlier, at the bar mitzvah of my son Teo Grossman, a conversation took place between Ron Kalom, Roger Lerman, Ted Dimond, Bruce Ross, and me about our experiences in studying the Torah. The spark came from Ron, who suggested that we meet and try to form a minyan to formally pray, honor the Sabbath, and then study. Using the old Reform prayer book *Gates of Prayer*, the journey began.

Every Saturday morning, we met around a table filled with books and random pieces of paper that had notes people brought or had jotted down as we studied. Different traditions started to take hold. The official service was called for 9 a.m., but more often than not a small group would arrive earlier, at 7:30, to socialize or discuss the week's events. Sometimes it was personal; a celebration, a new job, an illness in the family, or worse—a death. But usually it was a conversation about the political climate, something in Rwanda or Bill Clinton's fall from grace.

Yet somehow, miraculously, whatever we talked about led back to the Torah. As the appointed time arrived, Ron would stand up, a signal that we were about to begin. At some point he came up with a small chime—a perfectly tuned aluminum tube that he'd tap with a small mallet, and it would evoke an arresting sound that focused everyone.

Then we would begin our service, always with the *Mah Tovu* prayer: Mis-ke-no-te-cha Yisrael (How lovely are your tents, O Jacob, your dwellings, O Israel.), Numbers 24:5.

I'm not certain where the melody for the prayer we sang originated, but it was hauntingly beautiful and set a tone for the rest of the service. This ancient prayer itself can be traced back to the first known *siddur,* compiled by Rav Amram Gaon in the ninth century. The section of the Torah whence the words are taken is one of the few comical moments in the holy scripture. The lines are from the portion "Parashat Balak," where the Moabite King, Balak, hires a local prophet/oracle,

Balaam, to place a curse on the neighboring Israelite tribes. Instead of a curse, out came these enchanting lines that have endured for centuries.

The symbolism is not lost in considering the small miracle that a minyan was created and flourished in the Jewish wilderness of Taos. What might have been a curse on Jewish life in a place devoid of any traditional structure or guidance produced a spontaneous and heartfelt group of supplicants.

The weeks and years rolled forward. We met in each other's homes and then shared a bagel brunch together with great frivolity. Word got out that there was the little group that met every Saturday and something special was taking place. No membership, no fees, no rabbi; anyone interested in prayer and study was welcome.

The names of all those who came and went are too numerous to recall. In addition to the original six of us, the early attendees included Roberta Lerman, Hank Saxe, Cynthia Patterson, Norman and Dana Auftertig, Gary Schiff, Robert Pasternack, Herb Rachelson, Carmi Plaut, Susan Berman, Sue Anne Lasker, and many others. Over the almost twenty years that the minyan existed, hundreds of people came and went. When asked, "Who is in the Taos Minyan?" Ron Kalom would always reply, "Whoever is present on any given Sabbath." To this day, most who attended hold those minyan moments close to their hearts as an irreplaceable and transformative experience.

After meeting in people's homes for a couple of years, Ron Kalom made arrangements with Art and Jenny Greeno, proprietors of the Apple Tree Restaurant, to use their upstairs space for the services. It was located on Bent Street, the current site of Lambert's Restaurant. At the time, the Apple Tree opened for lunch at noon, so the deal was that we could use the upstairs room overlooking the small courtyard facing the street from 7:30 until 11:30 every Saturday morning. No charge.

The new venue altered the nature of the group. Meeting in the privacy of people's homes offered an open-ended intimate setting and also kept what was happening private and away from the public. Now that the minyan gathered in downtown Taos at one of the more prominent eateries in the county, its presence became more public.

During the warmer months, we opened the windows, allowing the cool breezes to waft through the small room that could easily overheat from the exuberant energy of the minyanites. Just below the window there was an espresso coffee cart and tables for patrons to sip their lattes and munch on pastries. The sonorous sounds of our prayers filled the little courtyard.

We never had any complaints, and in fact, it was not uncommon for vacationing Jews to hear the familiar liturgical chants and find their way upstairs to discover a remarkable sight, a crowd of wayward Jews praying to honor the Sabbath. The curious onlookers sometimes just gawked, smiled, and left. If they stayed, one of us would inevitably step out into the doorway and briefly explain our presence and welcome them to join. On many occasions they came right in and were handed a *siddur,* and they became new minyan members, at least for that day.

There is a point toward the end of the service when, in traditional congregations, the actual Torah scroll is taken out of the ark, paraded around the congregants, then opened to the portion and read by one or more people in Hebrew. In the beginning, the minyan had no scroll (that would come later). Instead, we had several different translations of the Torah, ranging from the Orthodox Art Scroll edition to the traditional Hertz Chumash to the version that Carmi Plaut's uncle, Gunther Plaut, edited for the Reform denomination. There were other versions as well.

After we said the introductory prayers for the reading of the Torah, we went around the room, each person reading a paragraph or two that was prefaced by saying what edition they were reading from. In this way, we covered all the Jewish bases and interpretations. This wasn't by design, but the result was a mosaic of translations covering all the traditions. Each edition had its own commentaries, and often people did research during the week that offered additional insights from sources such as Nehama Leibowitz, Joseph Ber Soloveitchik, and Abraham J. Twerski; others found information from the internet or elsewhere. All were invited to have their turn at the plate and swing away at what moved or angered or captivated them on any given Saturday.

As far as any of us knew, including Ron, nothing like this had ever happened before, at least not in this way. A structure existed with the prayers and the reading of the weekly portion, but once the discussion began, a barrage of free-flowing ideas and reactions burst across the table.

Questions held sway during the exploration of the text. Ron set the tone early on by declaring that there were no stupid questions; even the most naïve query was addressed respectfully and with deference. After all, we were all seekers in search of something that had eluded us. Some had more education in the tradition than others, but it never mattered because, once we took our place around the table, each person's voice was as valid as the other. Oftentimes, contemporary or personal events—like the assassination of Yitzhak Rabin or a story about someone's Aunt Lena, who survived the Holocaust—were pitched into the fray. Sometimes, it added to and enriched the discussion;

other times, it seemed tangential and didn't lead anywhere. But it didn't matter because there was always an authenticity to the nature of what we were doing that kept us moving along the path toward wisdom.

As 11:30 drew near, we closed our Torah translations and bookended the service by reciting the traditional blessing for completing the Torah reading. The final prayers of the morning were the *Aleinu* and the *Mourner's Kaddish*. Ron kept a copious list of people who had passed on, a *yahrzeit* list, which was part of a large calendar he kept at home. Each week, along the margin of the homily he'd prepared, he jotted down the names of people to be memorialized. His list included members of the Taos Jewish community, his own family, local community members, and historic figures, both Jewish and non-Jewish. So on any given Shabbat, his list might include Maimonides, Emerson, Chana Kalom (Ron's grandmother), and the Taos writer Frank Waters. This expansion of the traditional way *Kaddish* was used gave permission for the rest us to do the same. Before chanting the Mourner's Prayer, we went around the room and each person had the opportunity to say the names of those they wanted to honor.

I don't recall how Lou Kalish found his way to the minyan, but he showed up one day. Perhaps he heard us from the street. He prayed with us with great enthusiasm, knowing all the chants and melodies. When it came time for the Torah discussion, he became irritated and revealed his umbrage toward God, declaring himself an atheist. We were a bit stunned, wondering why he had come if he had no interest in God.

"Where was God when I was in the concentration camp?" he demanded. "Where was God when my whole family was slaughtered? There is no God and if there was one, I'd want no part of It."

The room fell silent as if a hand had throttled all our throats. Finally, I said, "I can understand that, but why bother to pray and sing these prayers if you don't have any faith?"

"My faith," Lou said, "is not with God, but with the Jewish people. I can't, I won't let their voices, their story, their history be silenced. My chants are for them and only them."

Lou showed up for the couple of weeks he vacationed here and then he was gone, but his commentary stayed with all of us who had met him, and his name was often invoked when we discussed the "hidden face of God." Was it possible to have faith without believing in an eternal supreme being? Yes, you could be like Lou Kalish.

Rabbi Jonathon Omer-Man came to the minyan one morning. Maybe two? I'm sure he was in Taos because of his connection with Rabbi Judith HaLevy. Whatever the reason, there he was sitting at the table talking and praying with us. Despite his stature as an esteemed rabbi and mystical scholar, Rabbi Jonathon joined the minyan just like the rest of us. In fact, he made it known that his primary interest in being there was to have the experience of being part of our minyan. Before leaving, he offered a brief discourse on the importance and relevance of a minyan from a historic and spiritual perspective: We are a kingdom of priests, and every Jew has the honor and responsibility to articulate their voice and offer their heartfelt connection to the tradition. His presence validated what we were doing.

Later, in conversation with Ron, he told him that he was moved by what we were doing in the little room at the Apple Tree Restaurant. And by the way, he added, if you are ever short of your required number of ten for the minyan, know that I will be with you on a spiritual level to make up the difference. He went on to explain in Kabbalist terms the notion of *tzimtzum*, which literally means contradiction. On the mystical level, in order to have made the world, God needed to conceal or remove "Itself" in order to have room for the universe to be created. "If your minyan doesn't have sufficient numbers on Shabbat, I will fill the void. Know that my presence will always be with you."

I believe the spirit of Rabbi Omer-Man always was in the room with us.

Years later, another well-known Rabbi made his way up the steps of the Apple Tree Restaurant. As I recall, Rabbi Michael Schudrich, an American serving as the current Chief Rabbi of Poland, was on a research project funded by the Ronald S. Lauder Foundation. It must have been in the late '90s, because he was living in Warsaw but did not have any rabbinic responsibility while he worked for the Lauder Foundation. In 2000, he was appointed Rabbi of Warsaw and Lodz and received his appointment as Chief Rabbi of Poland in 2004.

I don't recall how he found his way to the minyan. My recollection is walking in one morning and he was sitting next to Ron, chatting about his research regarding the converso Jews of Northern New Mexico. I sat down and listened to his story about his connection with Ron Lauder, his abiding interest in Poland, and that country's lack of any Jewish or rabbinic presence, which had remained decimated since the Holocaust.

Like Rabbi Omer-Man, the Conservative rabbi only wished to join the minyan for the day and partake with everyone else. Naturally, we were all fascinated with his story and his ambitions to revive the presence of Judaism in Poland. What still amazes me about his visit was his humility and accessibility. After the service, he invited a few of us out to lunch, where we continued the conversation about his research in New Mexico and his experiences in Poland.

The minyan rolled along, meeting every Saturday morning, always with a different combination of faces and stories. Often, something novel happened, but one morning, in early February of 1996, a very serendipitous event took place. Ron told the group that he had received a call from Taos artist Larry Bell informing him that the oddest thing had occurred. An eccentric, formerly wealthy Jewish man, Bryan Deutsch, who was living north of town, had found his way to Larry's studio and deposited piles of esoteric, antique Jewish books on his table, hoping that somehow Larry could take them off his hands.

Ron rushed over and examined the stash. Many were museum quality, dating back to the sixteenth and seventeenth centuries, but Ron determined that none of them had any viable use for the Taos Minyan. However, Bryan had told Larry that he also had a small authentic Torah that might be of interest. That did pique Ron's interest.

On Sunday, February 4, Ron, Roger, Hank, Cynthia, and I visited Bryan at his home. He had been living in a palatial residence in Valdez for a few years, having moved here because he loved to ski. Bryan explained that his family business had consisted of renting thousands of stock photographs that were used for all types of commercial ventures, but digital photography had virtually bankrupted the enterprise, so now he was in desperate financial straits and, sadly, had to sell his collection of Jewish books. He told us that he was a scholar of ancient Hebrew texts and had participated in several traditional Jewish Courts—Beit Din.

We made it clear that while his antique book collection was exquisite, it was more appropriate for a museum or university. We thanked him. Roger asked if we could please take a look at the Torah scroll.

Bryan nodded and said, "Yes. Of course."

A Torah in Valdez, New Mexico? How was this possible? We followed him into his library. The little Torah was sitting alone at the far end of a long table. Bryan lifted it as if it were a small doll. It was draped in a frayed linen cover that looked tired and neglected. Now unveiled, the scroll revealed itself to the last portion that had been read, Vayakhel, Exodus 35, where G-d commands the people to build an ark. It also happened that February 4, 1996, coincided with the portion Yitro, Exodus 18, wherein the Hebrew people made the Sinai pledge *Na'aseh V'Nishma,* and accepted the Decalogue, "All that the Lord has spoken, we will do."

Bryan estimated the little Torah to be about 150 years old, and it probably came from Germany. Somehow it had escaped the Holocaust. According to Bryan, a small Sefer Torah like this would have been owned by a pious Jew who used it when he traveled, a kind of "laptop Torah."

"If this had been a couple years ago," Bryan said, "I would have just given you this Torah, but now I'm afraid I must get some monetary reimbursement."

Standing around the table and looking at the Torah, we all felt a similar sense of responsibility, as if we had suddenly come across an orphaned child alone in the wilderness. Certainly, this wasn't Sinai, yet there we stood under Taos Mountain before a holy scroll. No way were we going to leave Valdez without it. After an hour of discussing terms and conditions, the little Torah was delicately loaded into the car.

Later that year, Bruce Ross transported it to Chicago, where Rabbi Moshe Shaingarten, a certified *sofer*, repaired and authenticated the little Torah. Roberta Lerman made the blue velvet cover that currently protects the parchment. It remains a living, vibrant part of our Taos Jewish history. When the minyan stopped meeting several years ago, the Torah was given to the Taos Jewish Center, where it remains safe and ready for the next service.

Ron kept the Torah at his house in a cedar ark that Roger had built. Every Saturday morning, he carried it up the steps and placed it in the center of the table. Sometimes we read directly from it during the services and sometimes we didn't, but we always made sure it was rolled to the correct portion for the week. Suddenly, the wayward Jews of the Taos Minyan had the serious responsibility of honoring and guarding an authentic Torah scroll. Because of its size, it was easily transported, and from time to time, it was used for bar/bat mitzvah or for individual study.

When the Taos Jewish Center was founded in 2002, the minyan, along with B'nai Shalom and the Sunday school—led by Roger Lerman, Lisa Guttmann, and Jean Schumer—became charter members and were given free use of the space. The minyan numbers grew, because the services were being held in a community space and notice was given to all the members of the TJC. Meetings were held in the library, so now the group was surrounded by more commentaries and resource materials, including two sets of the Talmud that had been donated. The energy and involvement grew so that, often, more than twenty people squeezed around the table in the Taos Jewish Center library. The little Torah resided inside a safe at the TJC, along with the other, larger, Holocaust Torah that belonged to B'nai Shalom.

The minyan met regularly until 2014. During the last few years, Ron Kalom's health began to decline and his regular attendance diminished until, one day, he no longer had the energy to attend. For a while others took a leadership role, but none could match his consistent presence, and numbers slowly declined until there was only a handful of people attending. Sadly, after almost twenty years, the minyan stopped meeting. While none of the attendees had come to Taos to be Jewish, for most of them the experience will remain an exquisite and unique memory.

The Taos Jewish Center

"The cloud covered the Tent of Meeting, and the glory of Hashem filled the Tabernacle."
—Exodus 40:34

"In My house and within My walls I will give them a place of honor and renown."
—Isaiah 56:5

For many years, members of the Jewish community had voiced the need for a Jewish space in Taos. B'nai Shalom Havurah was meeting in people's homes or rented space for the High Holidays. The Taos Minyan met at the Apple Tree Restaurant and held their High Holiday gatherings at the community room in the Taos Public Library or at Stables Gallery. Meanwhile, the B'nai Shalom Sunday School was also meeting in individual residences. In addition, a Jewish library existed under the auspices of B'nai Shalom, but there wasn't any public space for that either.

One Shabbat afternoon after our minyan services, a group of us went on a hike up to Devisadero Peak. About halfway up the mountain, an idea jolted me.

Perhaps the three existing Jewish groups could join together and lease a space for Jewish worship, study, and education. No one group alone could do it, but possibly if we joined together it could work. When we stopped at the top I revealed my idea. Actually, I might have started talking about it before we reached the top. Nonetheless, there was some interest, and I let it percolate for a few weeks. Could this really work? The personalities and Jewish backgrounds of Taos Jews were as varied as river rocks in the Rio Grande, but the idea of a Jewish place might pull all the rolling stones into one stable foundation.

At the time, Roger Lerman, Lisa Guttmann, and Jean Schumer were running the Sunday school. Roger thought the idea might work, as did Lisa and Jean. A place to permanently store their books and materials would be a godsend. I knew from attending a meeting with B'nai Shalom Havurah that there were many members voicing the idea of a Jewish space. I knew Beth Goldman from the minyan, and I knew she was a respected member of B'nai Shalom. I thought she would be the right person to float the idea about gathering the tribes under one tent.

It was right around Hanukkah of 2001 when I approached Beth while she was participating at the Millicent Rogers Museum's Holiday Fiesta. B'nai Shalom put together a booth with games and food, and Beth was in charge. In between dreidel games with groups of giggling Taos kids, I unpacked my idea about a collaborative Jewish space. Beth thought it could work and volunteered to approach B'nai Shalom with the idea.

A meeting took place at the Taos Bakery in the spring of 2002. Interestingly, the bakery was on Gusdorf Road, just north of where the TJC is currently situated. The owners were Israeli and were more than happy to allow a group of Jews to use the space for the purposes of an organizational start-up meeting. Carmi Plaut was instrumental in getting the word out to the community, and the fervor in the air was palpable. It didn't hurt that the bakery was renowned for its bread, pastries, and savory food. I think that as time goes by, I mentally increase the number of people who attended that initial meeting, so now I imagine it was between eighty and a hundred. It could have been sixty, or even fifty. What matters is that the Jewish souls present were excited and willing to take the plunge into making a real Jewish place in Taos. The notion *We can do this* permeated the air inside the room.

Events moved quickly after that, and the Taos Jewish Center was formally dedicated at a ceremony on September 1, 2002. After many years of wandering in the high desert, Taos Jews finally had a place where the three groups could meet, the B'nai Shalom library could be housed, and the B'nai Shalom Torah could rest.

Great excitement and energy abounded when the TJC opened. A board of directors was elected and Carmi Plaut was the first president. The Jewish Federation of New Mexico and the New Mexico Jewish Historical Society honored the new organization during the first few years. I became the second president after a few months, and suddenly, I felt energized and amazed. A kind of Jewish tidal wave swept over me.

In the beginning, the vision was for it to be a space where other existing groups would gather and do their "Jewish thing," while the board of the TJC would maintain and finance the space through donations and fundraising. Several generous donations helped provide a start for the organization. Soon memberships were added, which helped create financial stability but also made the distinction between members and nonmembers. Unfortunately, that isolated some people, although the board has always striven to make membership affordable to anyone who wanted to become a member.

The first few years in the organization's life were filled with a great deal of idealism and energy. Collaboration between the existing Jewish groups fueled the early engine that produced a strong board with an abundance of enthusiasm. Within the first year of its inception, the place where no one came to be Jewish transformed into a virtual Jewish renaissance.

In the winter of 2003, the first issue of the TJC newsletter was printed. Listed in that initial bulletin were twelve different Jewish groups, including Hadassah, The Chesed Project, Chabad (not the current version but something Jonathan Sobol offered in conjunction with the Santa Fe group), B'nai Shalom, Taos Minyan, Taos Havurah (a group Carmi Plaut started with some friends), and the New Mexico Kosher Co-op. In addition, a formal Jewish library was founded at the TJC under the auspices of Roger Lerman. It represents a valuable collection that had been donated to B'nai Shalom over the years but never had a permanent public home. At the present time, according to William Westbury, who now administers the library, there are over 2,500 titles.

The board quickly realized that there was a need for someone to guide and manage the programs, caretake the facility, and coordinate the fundraising necessary to keep the doors open and the utilities paid. A search was initiated, and the position of a part-time director was advertised. After interviewing several candidates from around the state, it became clear to the board that Beth Goldman, who was one of the founders and a board member at the time, was the most qualified for the position. Beth not only had a background in organizational work, but her human relations skills, as well as her background in Judaism and her knowledge of the Taos community, made her the perfect choice to lead the TJC. It was sad to lose her as an active member of the board, but what the TJC gained with Beth as the director was invaluable. She provided the necessary leadership for the first decade of the TJC and, without her drive and excitement, many of the TJC programs would not have been possible.

Peace Chanukah was one of the first innovative programs the TJC initiated. It was 2002 and the first time Hanukkah was celebrated at TJC. Carmi Plaut heard about Peace Chanukah from a Jewish group in Chicago that wanted to bring Jews and Palestinians together for a winter celebration. He recounted how it all started in an article in the TJC newsletter in the winter of 2012:

> The TJC was still in its infancy. Our vision was to create an event where many beliefs and faiths came together to celebrate a common theme. These included Christian, Hindu, Buddhist, Muslim, and Sikh groups, and members of the Taos Pueblo, as well as other Native Americans. Our first programming committee did not want Peace Chanukah to be a political event; instead, we wanted a statement about bringing light into the world during the darkest time of the year.

Our goal in those early days of the TJC (and also now) was to bring together people of different faiths and find common spiritual ground. The key word was SHARE. We wanted to have local spiritual leaders and speakers share words, prayers, songs and, of course, share chocolate *gelt* (not chocolate guilt). Most importantly, we wanted to share LIGHT. We all lit menorahs. During the Peace Chanukah we shared "togetherness" in our words of hope and SHALOM. Peter Wengert built a large menorah that honored speakers, and at that first Peace Chanukah we had over fifty menorahs ablaze with light. What a sight, what a spiritual gathering!

Twenty years have passed since that first celebration, and Peace Chanukah continues to be celebrated. It has evolved into a communal event, sponsored by the Taos Jewish Center, B'nai Shalom, and the Enchanted Circle Interfaith Gathering. Many members of the Jewish community who were initially involved included Bonnie Korman, Roy and Sharon Sharfin, Beth Goldman, and many others. Bette Myerson has been instrumental in helping keep the tradition alive. At the present time, it is believed that Taos is the only place still celebrating a Peace Chanukah.

Communication is vitally important to any organization, and shortly after its inception, the TJC board realized they needed to get program information out to members. Karl Halpert, a TJC board member, musician, and local entrepreneur, volunteered to begin a newsletter. He decided to call it *HaKol*—"the voice" in Hebrew. It began as a humble but well-constructed bulletin with general information about programs and brief editorials by board members, staff, and, of course, the editor. Karl did a tremendous job putting out quarterly issues that kept the community informed, involved, and interested.

My stepdaughter, Emily Sadow, helped with the initial layout for the first couple of years. Then in 2004, Susan Ressler, a TJC member and retired photography professor in the art department at Purdue University, signed on as associate editor. An acclaimed photographer, Susan's keen eye and aesthetic sensitivity miraculously changed the newsletter into a handsome professional journal. The new format was an 8.5×11-inch exquisitely printed tour de force that included masterful articles and photographs. Karl's cousin Joanna Kraus, an award-winning playwright and author, also joined as a regular contributor. *HaKol* continued to thrive under Halpert and Ressler. In the winter of 2010, after eight illustrious years at the helm, Karl and Susan stepped down. During their tenure, the quality of the articles and visual impact of the journal were unsurpassed. They were a part of what seemed to me to be a golden age of Jewish life in Taos. Those first eight years were filled with extraordinary programs, personalities, and excitement.

For a few years, I did my best to fit into Karl's shoes as editor, with the help of Beth Levine, Jim Levy, Jay Levine, and Roberta Lerman. In the Winter 2010 issue, Karl and Susan wrote their farewell pieces, worthy of reading. Copies of all the *HaKol*s are available in the TJC library. The current version, edited by the multi-talented Karen Kerschen, is now an online magazine, free of the restraints of printing and postage costs. It also offers endless room for art, photography, and extensive stories and articles. Because of the internet accessibility at TJC, members can link onto lectures, podcasts, and plays.

The first year, the board was not quite sure how to handle the High Holidays. Should they hire a rabbi? The Taos Minyan had always done its own service, as had B'nai Shalom. Now both groups were using the same space, so what to do? A collaboration between the groups took place and was perhaps one of the most satisfying experiences the community had ever had. Ron Kalom, Naomi Hannah, and others led the service. That lasted only for the first year, and by 2004, the services were led by Rabbi Lewis (Buz) Bogage, the university rabbi and director of Jewish Studies at DePauw University. Naomi Hannah assisted as the designated *chazzan* for the service.

The following year, Rabbis Arthur Waskow and Phyllis Berman (Waskow's wife and partner) led the services at the Fort Burgwin campus of SMU. Both of these famed spiritual leaders expressed an enthusiastic interest in coming to Taos to lead services. Taos was probably well-known to them because of their connection to the Renewal leader Rabbi Zalman Schachter-Shalomi, who had spent time at the Lama Foundation. Waskow had already authored several books, the most famous being *Godwrestling*, published in 1987. He was the founder of the Shalom Center, a foundation dedicated to world peace. Its mission was to "equip activists and spiritual leaders with awareness and skills needed to lead in shaping a transformed and transformative Judaism that can help create a world of peace, justice, healing for the earth, and respect for the interconnectedness of all life." Rabbi Berman co-authored several books with her husband and was the founder of the Riverside Language Program for immigrants and refugees in New York City. Taos, the place where no one came to be Jewish, attracted many esteemed rabbis.

Famous as they were, Waskow and Berman were not congregational rabbis; so the next year, the TJC Board decided to search for a rabbi who could commit to Taos for more than a single year. A search committee was formed and, much to the surprise of the group, several worthy candidates expressed interest in becoming a part-time rabbi for the Taos Jewish Center.

Diminutive in stature but large in heart and mind, Rabbi David Stein stood out among the many commendable applicants. Already famous for his scholarly editorial work in Judaic studies—including "The Contemporary Torah: A Gender-Sensitive Adaptation of the JPS [Jewish Publication Society] Translation"; "The Torah: Documentation for the Revised Edition of the Torah: A Modern Commentary," published by the Union for Reform Judaism; and the preface to the "JPS Hebrew-English Tanakh"—Rabbi Stein held an abiding interest in and curiosity about being in community with other Jews. His eclectic background included studying engineering at Arizona State and Stanford; he later attended the Reconstructionist Rabbinical College in Philadelphia and, after that, held a position as a congregational rabbi at a small synagogue in Baltimore. In his spare time, Rabbi David sang in a barbershop quartet, rode his bike along the beach, and engaged in the martial art of aikido. David had the right kind of off-beat mixture that appealed to the Taos Jewish community. Quiet, unassuming, brilliant, and insightful, his love of the natural world, coupled with his incisive knowledge of all spectra of Judaism, from the most ancient to the most contemporary, made him a great fit for the TJC's first regular rabbi. In his interview with Karl Halpert in the fall of 2006, he described his relationship to Reconstructionism and Judaism:

> Because a certain traditional practice or restriction has been redemptive in the past, we assume that it still has the potential to be redemptive. We study it in community to see how doing it might make sense in our own time and place. After trying honestly to let Jewish tradition speak to us with regard to the meanings and functions of the matter in question, and seeing how it might be important for other Jews, we may decide to adopt that practice or restriction for ourselves. Or we may decide that it's not for us, preferring that the same functions be carried out in other ways. Either way, integrity comes from the process of engagement. Thus, we treat our traditions with respect while creatively renewing them.

During the six years that Rabbi Stein served at the Taos Jewish Center, his High Holiday Services were emblematic of his philosophy. The Days of Awe became an opportunity for anyone who wished to be involved, deeply involved, to take part. The TJC hiring committee became the "ritual committee," whose job it was to fill all the traditional slots that the rabbi had allotted, from Torah readers and carriers to members of a chorus to readers and greeters, so that the holiday became almost operatic in its scale and involvement. During his term as rabbi, many in the community had their first authentic relationship with traditional Jewish rituals surrounding the Torah and the liturgy. David Stein and his wife, Carol, became endearing and lasting members of the Taos Jewish community.

Unintentionally, Rabbi Stein's article in *HaKol* in the fall of 2006 coincided with the arrival of The Kotzker de Taos. In The Kotzker's inaugural article, called "For the Sake of Heaven," the opening lines were:

> A rabbi in Taos? Surely, you're yanking my *peyos* (sideburns). A rabbi in Taos: unlikely as a *tzaddik in pelz* (a righteous one in fur). But surely, a fiddler on the roof was even crazier until Marc Chagall actually made it happen. Of course it's crazy. The times could not be more *meshuggah*. And in Taos, all the more so. So what do we have here—Anatevka in the Southwest? Could be. After all, we pray a lot, and prayer makes more happen than we care to admit.

No one came to Taos to be Jewish, yet the era of a regular rabbi at the Taos Jewish Center had begun, and The Kotzker, of all people, heralded the beginning. Six years was a long time for David and Carol to sojourn from Los Angeles to Taos. It was time for another voice to take the Taos stage.

In September of 2012, Rachel Kolman, a friend and TJC member, called and invited Cindy and me to a dinner gathering at the San Geronimo Lodge. The San G, as it was commonly known, had been a meeting place for many important Jewish events. Rachel and her mother belonged to Chavurat Hamidbar (The Fellowship of the Desert) in Albuquerque. This group, founded in 1973, held annual retreats, and that year it was in Taos. The guest speaker was Rabbi Paul Citrin. Rabbi Citrin had been the rabbi at Congregation Albert for 18 years before leaving in 1996. He and his wife, Susie, returned to Albuquerque when he retired in 2011. Paul delivered a stirring lecture about a Jewish poet, which was intellectually and spiritually stimulating. Afterward Rachel introduced Cindy and me not only to Rabbi Paul but also to her cousins Dr. Neal and Diane Friedman, who at the time were part-time residents in Taos. Later, they would move to Taos and become active in the TJC. Neal served as president of the board for several years and has remained on the board. Paul and Susie loved Taos, and our initial conversation drifted into talks about hiking trails and the abundant wilderness in the area. They shared a fantasy of someday having a place in Taos. One subject led to another, and soon we were talking about the TJC and our need for a part-time rabbi. The synchronicity of Rabbi Citrin's recent retirement and the desire of the TJC to have a regular rabbinic presence was stunning. It didn't take the board long to make the decision to hire Paul as the first congregational rabbi. The plan was for him to come once a month, conduct Friday-night services followed by a Saturday morning class with the children of the B'nai Shalom school, and finally, a Torah study and a *kiddush* (blessing).

Rabbi Paul Citrin and Rabbi David Stein were quite different in their approaches to leading a congregation. Rabbi Paul was a relaxed, warm jokester, whereas Rabbi David was more reserved but loved to sing, and music was very important to him. Surprisingly, the link between the two was Cindy Grossman. It was Rabbi David who first invited Cindy to share the *bimah* during the High Holidays and encouraged her to learn new aspects of the liturgy. During the six years that Rabbi David conducted services, Cindy became a full participant during the holidays, harmonizing with him, playing the guitar, or doing particular prayers on her own. Although trained as a classical singer and having substituted for cantors when she lived in Boston,

Las Vegas, and Santa Fe, this was the first time she'd had a regular position with a congregation.

When Rabbi Paul took the reins, one of his initial acts was to claim Cindy as *mein kantor*. Always the showman, Rabbi Paul would make a big deal about sharing the spotlight with Cindy. For her, it was almost embarrassing but, on the other hand, she said she felt validated and fully supported in the role of cantor for the first time. Paul's trust and encouragement motivated her to study and practice at a higher level. Now, in her cantorial career, she felt a sense of authenticity as a prayer leader.

Cindy grew up in a conservative Jewish family. Her mother, also a singer, had often sung solo parts in their temple's choir. Two great uncles on her mother's side were cantors who'd perished during the Holocaust. In asking her about her career as a cantorial soloist, she shared a poignant story about when she substituted for the cantor at Congregation Ner Tamid in Las Vegas, Nevada. Before the service, she and Rabbi Sandy Akselrad met in a room behind the sanctuary. After going over the service, he wrapped his *tallit* around her and said a few prayers in order to help her hold the sacred space. During those few moments she realized the gravitas of chanting the ancient prayers of the Jewish people.

Cindy didn't come to Taos to be Jewish or to be a cantor. She came to ski. But in 2000 she had a serious skiing accident and fell 150 feet into rocks and trees. Miraculously, she was not seriously injured. "The mountain," she said, "wanted me to do other things. In retrospect, I guess it wanted me to chant the liturgy, and when I chant High Holiday prayers now, I remember Sandy Akselrad and his *tallit* draped over me, and I channel my mother, my uncles, and all the generations that came before me. I have such gratitude." Cindy continues to serve as the TJC cantorial soloist under the leadership of Rabbi Judith HaLevy. Each year offers new challenges and opportunities and, with the help of "the mountain," Cindy continues to find the inspiration to sing with her heart and soul.

Rabbi Citrin brought professional "creds" to the Taos Jewish Community. Along with his exuberant energy and his ever-present wit, Paul had a powerful résumé as a congregational rabbi, having served in Boston, San Diego, Las Cruces, Philadelphia, and Albuquerque. Coincidentally, Paul and I attended UCLA at the same time; while I was figuring out my future in San Francisco, Paul was attending the Hebrew Union College in Los Angeles, where he was ordained in 1973. While at Congregation Albert in Albuquerque, he co-founded the Jewish-Catholic Dialogue of New Mexico Inc. and served on the board of the Dr. Martin Luther King Jr. Multicultural Celebration for more than a decade. Committed to social justice and democratic rights, many of his sermons involved the deep connection between Judaism and social and environmental responsibility. He often evoked the concept of *tikkun olam* as a theme. In this way he was perfectly aligned with the liberal-leaning Taos population. Paul had a natural gift in relating to children and making learning fun and relevant to their developmental level. Through his efforts, the Sunday school (held on Saturday) flourished, although the number of students was far less than what Paul was accustomed to in the large urban congregations.

Trained as a Reform rabbi, Paul had experience with Jews with differing levels of knowledge of Hebrew and Jewish liturgy. Taos, however, was even more of an extreme, partly because no one came here to be Jewish, and many members of the TJC had never had any previous experience with the traditions. He made sure that prayers included transliteration of the Hebrew text and would "allow for modern interpretations as well as moments of silence."

In a *Taos News* interview, he described his role this way: "It's not a matter of trying to please everyone all the time; it's a matter of striking a balance. More than that, it's having an openness to this broad spectrum and approaching Judaism from a number of perspectives." Over the six years that Rabbi Citrin served, the TJC evolved into a more spiritually cohesive community, mostly because of the traditional services Paul conducted on a monthly basis. It was the first time such consistency had taken place so that children and families could experience Jewish life together. Before every Friday-night service, a community potluck was held, so there was also an element of social solidarity starting to happen in the group.

Paul worked closely with the TJC board, offering his expertise in areas of membership, leadership, and community building. A dedicated supporter of the State of Israel, Rabbi Citrin shared many first-hand experiences of life in the Holy Land. Both he and Susie led annual trips to Israel to help educate and share the beauty and spirituality of Israel. Through his direct knowledge of the country, along with his in-depth education, he was able to help the TJC community understand and appreciate the unique nature of our homeland.

In addition to his rabbinic and community work, Paul also found time to write. He has published four books. *Ten Sheaves* is a collection of sermons and articles. *Lights in the Forest* is a collection of responses by rabbis to twelve essential Jewish questions that he compiled and edited. *I Am My Prayer* is a memoir and personal exploration of his experience of prayer over the years. *Gates of Repentance for Young People* was co-edited by him and Judith Abrams.

After six solid years, Paul decided it was time to retire, this time for good (maybe). Currently, when he is not writing, praying, or teaching, Paul can be found walking or biking along the bosque in Albuquerque.

There have been many unique programs and activities at the TJC. Along with Peace Chanukah, one of the more incomparable ones was the Chesed Project. *Chesed* is a Hebrew word meaning loving kindness. Founded in 2003, the Chesed Project was established to work in collaboration with other community agencies and congregations to "break through the barriers of isolation and loneliness by providing services and activities for people age 60 and over, to increase independence and interdependence, to make seniors aware of community resources and services."

The story behind the Chesed Project can be traced back to when the Taos Minyan was still meeting at the Apple Tree. An elderly woman began wandering into the group, usually with a crumpled stack of papers. She would sit quietly for fifteen or twenty minutes, then begin speaking in a disassociated, halting cadence about events that had nothing to do with Torah or our discussion. It was usually a paranoid set of ramblings about being abused, abducted, and terrorized that ended with her getting hysterical and crying. After this happened a few times, we learned how to calm her down, and she was able to settle back into the flow of the liturgy, sitting quietly, and then leaving before the end of the service. Somehow I discovered that she had a son in the area, who was able to help her for a while; but she obviously needed serious professional intervention.

I knew that while her situation was extreme, there were other Jewish people in the community who could benefit from social services. I was aware that there was a Jewish Family Service of New Mexico office in Albuquerque, and I contacted them. At the time, Art Fine was the executive director. I made my case that the organization purported to serve Jews throughout the state, but in fact it really just provided services to Albuquerque and Santa Fe. We needed some assistance in Taos, and I told him the story of our troubled minyan member. He sympathized with our plight, and for a while, we dialogued about possibilities. He put me in touch with the social workers on his staff. Funding was tight and his outreach workers were overwhelmed with their local cases, so not much happened. I continued to make my case for assistance for the next year. In 2003, I received a call from Art. He said that he wasn't going to be able to send an outreach worker to Taos, but he had just received word that federal monies would be available through President Bush's new "Faith Based Initiative," and he was pretty certain that the TJC would be eligible for funding.

A state and federal partnership was formed called the Stone Soup Collaborative, and through that, funding was awarded to the TJC. The first director, Susan Hale, was an immensely talented and dynamic woman whose background was in music therapy and writing. At the time she was hired, she had already published two books dealing with the mystical aspects of song and voice, titled *Song and Silence: Voicing the Soul;* and *Sacred Space, Sacred Sound.* A self-starter, Susan immediately unfurled a comprehensive, creative, and compassionate program for seniors. The fact that she was not Jewish did not really matter, since the focus and guidelines of the Chesed Project determined that all programs were open to people of all faiths. The TJC now had a larger presence in the greater community.

From the beginning, in July of 2003, the Chesed Project provided a wide array of free programs, staffed by talented and creative people that Susan brought onboard. There is a long list of names of people who taught workshops and supported Chesed. The initial group of teachers included Rose Gordon, Susie Verkamp, Michele Marien, Dianne Pola, Jean Ellis-Sankari, and Eliza Collins. There was tremendous support from community groups and individuals. An advisory board was established, with Phyllis Hotch, Lisa Guttmann, Catherine Guynes, and Diane Rivera serving as the first members. Other collaborators included the B'nai

Shalom Havurah, St. James Episcopal Church, the First Presbyterian Church, UNM Taos, Ancianos Senior Center, Plaza de Retiro, SOMOS, Golden Willow Retreat Center, and the Taos School of Massage.

After two years, Susan moved on to work on her writing and music career. Fortunately, the TJC found another dedicated and talented leader for the Chesed Project in Kathleen Burg. With a master's degree in art and education from Goddard College, and a strong background in writing and community service, Kathleen was able to take the reins of the Chesed Project and hone it into a loving, responsive program for elders and caregivers. Her dedication and talent in communicating, fundraising, and networking sustained the program. After the national funding and some of the grants run out, the TJC was no longer be able to support the Chesed Project. Kathleen, however found a way to keep it going as a viable and valuable asset in the Taos community. In 2008 Kathleen spawned "Artstreams," a program whose mission is "to provide an opportunity for caregivers to become better educated about dementia; healthy lifestyle choices to combat stress; how to use available resources; and how to involve other family members, friends and the Taos community as a resource."

Kathleen Burg and Susan Hale were not the only non-Jews to play an important role in the development of the Taos Jewish Center. Without doubt, Michael Scudder and Peter Wengert definitely did not come to Taos to be Jewish; yet these two men both served on the TJC Board, and Peter acted as interim director for a period of time after Beth Goldman left. Both men found their way to the TJC via their wives, vigorous Jewish women who were extremely active in the Taos Jewish community. Michael's spouse, Phyllis Landis, served on the board and was vice president when Cindy Grossman was president in 2008. Ziva Moyal, Peter's partner, was also on the board and taught chanting and Kabbalah classes in the community. A native of Israel, Ziva provided leadership and guidance on a variety of spiritual and intellectual levels.

Peter had an illustrious background in psychology and political science. He was one of the founding members of the Guilford Press, an esteemed publisher specializing in innovative books and research on psychology. The word *exuberance* best defines Peter's personality. Always smiling and energetic, he contributed in almost every area of the TJC, from Torah discussions to fundraising to membership, he cheerfully offered his hands and mind to develop the organization. He was one of the great examples of righteous non-Jews who helped create and sustain the Taos Jewish community.

In many ways, Michael Scott Scudder had similar attributes. Michael's background was in business and development. He was responsible for developing a sustainable business plan for the TJC, as well as coming up with the idea of a founding members' drive. Michael expounded on the unique quality of the TJC in an article in *HaKol* in 2006, saying,

> For me, an Irish American Indian, the Taos Jewish Center ironically means a great deal. It symbolizes, epitomizes, and exudes "family." It is a space where all are welcome: Jews, Hispanics, Native Americans, Anglos, African Americans, Asians. The TJC is a wonderful hodgepodge of peoples.

Michael died on June 30, 2017, and is buried in the Eretz Shalom Cemetery. I will always remember him as someone with keen insight, a man who used his Irish wit to warm the room, a man who viewed and adored the natural world through his Lakota eyes, and a man who expressed compassion in a soulful Jewish way. He cared deeply and worked hard to make the TJC a place that was open to all.

Speaking of presence, it is hard to imagine a more omnipresent Taos Jew than Richard Wallach. Like the rest of us, Richard did not come to Taos to be Jewish. He came to ski and to open Ultima Photo Images on Bent Street. If there is any Jewish happening in Taos and Richard is not out of town fighting fires, you will find him there. As soon as the TJC opened, Richard rolled up his sleeves and got involved. Not only was he one of the early board members, he has been and continues to provide handyman, computer, and video support whenever it is needed. He is also the main *shofar* (horn) blower and *hagbah* (Torah raiser) during the High Holidays. Over the years he has built tables, mounted movie screens, set up websites, and installed track lights. His greatest gift, however, is his abiding commitment to community. Whether Torah study or fundraising, Richard is always the first one who says *Hineni* (I am here) when something needs to be done. Richard is emblematic of the Jew who welcomes and accepts everyone in the Taos community.

Over the years the TJC has held many sterling programs, music events, lectures, and even a Jewish genealogy workshop. To list and describe them all would be more than I can do in this short book, but there is one exquisite event that still curls my toes and staggers my senses. In the summer of 2008, we received a call from Mary Burns. She and her husband, Jim, are longtime supporters of the Taos art and music community, as well as other worthy nonprofits. Mary said that Jim's brother-in-law, Leon Leyson, was visiting Taos and we might be interested in meeting him. Why? Because Leon was one of the fortunate Jews who was on "Schindler's List," and he wished to share his story with all who might be interested. Of course we would be interested.

June 13, 2008, was a Friday. As a group, we lit Shabbat candles, made a *Kiddush,* and shared a meal together. Leon ate with us, then moved to the front of the room to tell his story. Born Leib Lejzon in Narewka, Poland, on September 15, 1929, Leon began his life under the dark shadow of German fascism. In 1938, his family moved to Krakow to try to improve their economic situation. When Germany invaded Poland in 1939, life for Jews ended as they knew it, and soon Hitler's Nazis were rounding up families and placing them in urban ghettos. Fortunately, Leon's father and brother found work under the protection of Oskar Schindler. Later, young Leon joined the ranks of the lucky few. He became number 69128 on Schindler's famous list. Leon was so small he needed to stand on a box in order to complete his work. That box later became the title for his memoir, *The Boy on the Wooden Box*, published by Simon & Schuster after Leyson's death at age eighty-three, in 2013.

Mr. Leyson humbly but passionately told his tale about being thirteen years old and meeting the famous Oskar Schindler, a complex and sometimes irreverent man, who, along with his wife, took it upon himself to save over 1,000 Jews. Leyson was the youngest factory worker in Schindler's ceramic plant and was practically starving when he started work. Leyson recalled how Schindler, seeing his emaciated condition, made arrangements for him to receive double rations in order to thrive. The entrepreneur took kindly to the young boy and made sure he had proper care. He often referred to him as "little Lejzon." Leon spoke about the dreadful reality that surrounded the Jews of Poland as his friends and loved ones disappeared, one by one, until the only ones who survived were the Schindler's list Jews.

What a night it was. Leon was so self-effacing, honest, and soulful as he told about coming to America in 1949, then being drafted in 1951 during the Korean War, where he served as an engineer. Afterward, he received a degree in industrial arts and became a high school teacher at Huntington Park High School in Southern California for thirty-nine years until he retired in 1997. He never shared the story of his experience during the war until Spielberg's movie was released in 1993. With great modesty, he recalled how one day, some of the teachers were raving about the movie and he happened to mention that he was one of Schindler's workers. His colleagues were stunned and in awe, but Leon didn't think much about it. Word got out quickly, and soon he was being asked to speak, and newspapers wanted his story. From that point forward, Leyson took every opportunity to make his story known. I recall that night at the TJC when he shared a tearful moment of actually meeting his rescuer again, when Oskar Schindler visited Los Angeles in 1965. As he approached Schindler, Leon wasn't sure the man would recognize him, but Schindler did, saying, "Of course I know who you are. You are little Lejzon, the boy on the wooden box." Leon told how he immediately felt elated and relieved by his smile and recognition. The authenticity and warmth of his story was an unforgettable moment for those present at the TJC that night.

As of this writing, the TJC continues to flourish, thanks to the board, the current leadership of Rabbi HaLevy, and the membership. Without the commitment of the presidents, the TJC would not have survived. Carmi Plaut, myself, Lisa Guttmann, Cindy Grossman, Jay Levine, Gary Atias, Jude Goldman Nuñez, and Neal Friedman all served as leaders with *kavanah* (heartfelt intention). Gary, the current present, has served twice —a remarkable testament to his loyalty to the TJC. Jay has remained on the board for over a decade and continues to provide heaps of technical support during the virtual Shabbat and High Holiday services. The dozens of board members over the years are too numerous to name here, but their service made certain the TJC thrived. The gathering place for Jews in the Taos Valley continues to thrive, even though the physical place has been closed since the start of the COVID pandemic.

The Eretz Shalom Cemetery

Jewish tradition has always dictated that the first thing a community should do is create a proper cemetery. When the B'nai Shalom Havurah grew to about sixty-five families, under the leadership of Rabbi Chavah Carp, the questions arose: *What's next? Should we hire a rabbi? A cantor? Should we rent a space? Perhaps create a cemetery?* A survey was sent out to the Jewish community, and the resounding response was *We need a cemetery.*

Roger Lerman took the lead in searching out a space beginning in the early 1990s. But it wasn't until 1993 that land was secured. Hank Saxe, a well-known ceramic artist and supporter of Taos Jewish organizations, was intrigued with the notion of having a Jewish cemetery in Taos. As he tells it, "Roger put out the word. No one offered any property—to my surprise, since it seemed like there were plenty of well-off Jewish landowners and investors. Go figure. Given that no one else jumped up and raised their hand, it seemed like it was up to us to make a piece available."

Hank consulted with his father, David, and they agreed to make a gift to the Jewish Community. Steve Natelson made sure the transfer was made properly, in good legal form. The land deed went to B'nai Shalom, where it remains today. Hank's mother, Adele, had recently died, so David dedicated the gift of the land to B'nai Shalom in memory of Adele and Hank's sister Janet, who had died in childhood in 1963.

Located on the Llano Quemado mesa, the one-acre parcel has a noteworthy history. In the late '70s, the Saxe family bought a tract of land that was owned by Art Kay, who had built the airport on the mesa between Llano Quemado and Los Cordovas. Kay was a Jewish man who came to Taos from Winslow, Arizona, in the late 1940s and opened a sporting goods business. He was also a pilot in need of a landing strip for his plane, so he purchased a 240-acre parcel for that purpose. His wife, Selma, was Dr. Al Rosen's sister, so there was already family here.

Like so many areas in Taos, the Llano Mesa had been home to Pueblo people during the period between 1000 BCE into the 1300s. There are many remnants of pit houses around Art Kay's original acreage, including the space around Eretz Shalom Cemetery. These sites are identified by slightly raised mounds and flakes of stone tools, as well as potsherds around the area. It is presumed that these early locations were abandoned when the groups moved to the pueblo at Pot Creek, south of Talpa, and then to the current home of the Taos Pueblo, sometime around 1325.

The land was originally part of the Gijosa land grant and was divided into forty-acre parcels in 1908 as part of a real estate promotion—the Ranchos Orchard and Land Company. The scheme was to convert this high-desert environment into apple orchards, and a ditch was partially dug to bring water out of the stream above Talpa, the Rio Grande del Rancho. The project never reached fruition, and the land remained in much the same state as it is now—sagebrush and chamisa. Naturally, those who purchased the land no longer had much interest and wound up selling on the cheap or just allowing it to languish, losing it for back taxes. Art Kay bought six of those forty-acre plots.

Toward the end of his life, he sold off the 240 acres. His landing strip was replaced by the current Taos Municipal Airport, and most of the remaining land was divided into smaller parcels. Hank Saxe recalls that at the time of his family's purchase of the land,

> There was only one residence on the old airport, a hand-built adobe house dug into the ground, surrounded by a few hundred acres of sagebrush. A realtor talked up the last big parcel of Kay's to us. We drove out

to look at the property in the dead of winter, careening over the snow-packed road in the real estate agent's old black Cadillac, keeping the car moving briskly so the street tires didn't bog down in the snow. We weren't able to identify the corners of the property under the snow, but it didn't matter much, as the ground appeared pretty much the same wherever you looked. The agent said, "It's somewhere out there." After some back and forth my folks ended up purchasing the tract of land.

Once the land was committed to the Jewish community under the legal auspices of B'nai Shalom, it needed to be consecrated. Tradition dictates that the land had to be set aside for the sole purpose of a cemetery, and it was. A group consisting of B'nai Shalom members, including Rabbi Chavah Carp, and members of the Taos Minyan met at the site and performed a ritual of walking around the grounds seven times; the number seven mirrors the seven days of creation as well as the seven years of the Jewish agricultural cycle. We said prayers and chanted the *Shema*. Maybe we recited a few psalms; I don't recall. I do remember that my children were there. The seven revolutions around the area sanctified the space, but other traditions call for some kind of physical separation, a wall or a fence.

For several consecutive weeks, a group of us met at the cemetery grounds on Friday afternoon. We first gathered stones in wheelbarrows from around the property, then piled them in central locations. Next, we lined out the boundaries. Roger, being a developer and all-around handyman, was instrumental in this process. We leveled the area as best we could, using shovels and other hand tools, then mixed small batches of mortar. Ever so slowly and ineptly, we laid the stones around the perimeter. Having arbitrarily gathered the rocks, nothing was uniform, and stacking them was not always easy; yet we persevered until we actually had a very, very low stone wall around the entire area. At its highest point, the wall might have reached eighteen inches, although I'm probably stretching that number for the sake of the numerical significance of eighteen in Judaism, meaning *chai*—to life and good luck.

Once the ground was sanctified, Roger took on the responsibility for organizing the plots, as well as figuring out the physical and administrative technicalities for actually operating a cemetery. He did a tremendous amount of research and presented all he had learned to the B'nai Shalom board for approval. From that point until his untimely death in 2019, Roger managed everything that was involved with the cemetery, including the building of a small bench and a ramada, arranging for the burials, and making certain the grounds were cleaned and weeded; he even fashioned the plain pine coffins used for the interments. His trusted backup was Steve Natelson, who graciously volunteered to take over the responsibility of managing the cemetery after Roger passed.

No one came to Taos to be Jewish. Or, as my friend Karl suggested in his foreword, perhaps, on some mystical level, everyone arrived here for the very purpose of unfurling their Judaism. Take your choice. Whatever you might believe, the past four decades have transformed the Taos Jewish landscape into a remarkable and vital home. Not only is there a great variety of groups and leaders, there is also a final resting place for generations to come.

There is a beautiful Hebrew song, "L'dor Vador" (from generation to generation). I believe that, as a community, we have set that theme in motion here in Taos. I can almost hear the melody streaming down from Taos Mountain.

Acknowledgments

I thank my loving wife, Cindy, for her indomitable partnership and inspiration in helping manifest this story. Her support and encouragement during the writing of this book kept me going and fueled my spirit. Her thoughtful suggestions and careful edits assisted in the completion of the project. She also continues to provide not only leadership as a Taos Jewish Center board member, but her cantorial eloquence enthuses the community throughout the seasons.

My gratitude goes to Rabbi Chavah Carp and Rabbi Judith HaLevy, firstly for taking the time to share their stories, and also for generously offering the delicious morsels of their inner journeys that have so enriched the Taos Jewish community. Many thanks to Bette Myerson and Bonnie Korman for sharing their firsthand accounts of coming to Taos, as well as the backstory of B'nai Shalom. This narrative would not have been complete without the heartfelt details that were offered by Carolyn Kalom and Roberta Lerman about their beloved spouses, Ron Kalom and Roger

Lerman, who are no longer with us. Thanks to Bruce Ross—not only for being my Israeli traveling partner but also for giving me feedback regarding our shared years in the Taos Minyan. Ted Dimond helped prod my memory about the early minyan days and motivated me to keep going.

Toda raba to Karl Halpert, who generously agreed to pen the preface to this book, as well as support my early efforts at the Taos Jewish Center. His devoted friendship and incisive intellect have remained steadfast over the years.

Hank Saxe kindly unveiled the history of Eretz Shalom, the Taos Jewish cemetery. Without his knowledge, that story would not have been told. I also wish to thank him and his family for their donation of the land for the cemetery.

Thank you to my copy editor Helen Rynaski, whose sharp eyes cleaned, shaped, and pruned my original manuscript. Special thanks to Barbara Scott, whose "final eyes" and aesthetic mastery brought this project home.

Finally, my deepest appreciation to all the members of the Taos Jewish community, past and present, who have found a way to celebrate and honor Judaism in their own personal way. May their collaborative voices and memories continue to bless this valley, and may the light of Taos Mountain continue to shine into the hearts of all who come here to make this their dwelling place.

I express my gratitude to Susan Ressler for her insightful suggestions for this second edition.

About the Author

Born in Chicago but raised in Los Angeles, Bruce Grossman traveled in Europe after graduating from  UCLA in 1969. He worked as a teacher and a photographer in San Francisco until moving to Taos in 1976, where he continues to live and work as a psychotherapist. *We Go On Living*, his book of poetry about the death of his father, was published in 2007. *The Captive*, a novel about Sandy Koufax, awaits publication. He is married to pastel artist Cindy Grossman and has two sons, both born in Taos.

www.ingramcontent.com/pod-product-compliance
Lightning Source LLC
LaVergne TN
LVHW011421080426
835512LV00005B/186